THE LAST THINGS

The Last Things

BIBLICAL AND THEOLOGICAL
PERSPECTIVES ON ESCHATOLOGY

Edited by

Carl E. Braaten and Robert W. Jenson

William B. Eerdmans Publishing Company
Grand Rapids, Michigan / Cambridge, U.K.

Wm. B. Eerdmans Publishing Co.
255 Jefferson Ave. S.E., Grand Rapids, Michigan 49503 /
P.O. Box 163, Cambridge CB3 9PU U.K.

Printed in the United States of America

07 06 05 04 03 02   7 6 5 4 3 2 1

Library of Congress Cataloging-in-Publication Data

The last things: biblical and theological perspectives on eschatology /
edited by Carl E. Braaten and Robert W. Jenson.
      p.   cm.
    Includes bibliographical references.
    Contents: The task of Christian eschatology / Wolfhart Pannenberg —
The recovery of apocalyptic imagination / Carl E. Braaten — The great
transformation / Robert W. Jenson — Prophetic and apocalyptic politics /
Paul D. Hanson — Eschatology in the New Testament: the current debate /
Arland J. Hultgren — Law and eschatology: a Jewish-Christian intersection /
David Novak — The Book of Revelation and orthodox eschatology: the
theodrama of judgment / John A. McGuckin — Luther and the apocalypse:
between Christ and history / Philip D. W. Krey — Hints from science for
eschatology and vice versa / George L. Murphy.
    ISBN 0-8028-4878-8 (pbk.: alk. paper)
    1. Eschatology. 2. Eschatology — Biblical teaching.
I. Braaten, Carl E., 1929- II. Jenson, Robert W.

BT821.3.L37 2002
236 — dc21

                               2002023824

www.eerdmans.com

Contents

Preface

The twentieth century will be remembered in the history of theology for its rediscovery of the centrality of eschatology in the message of Jesus and early Christianity. But it reached no consensus on the shape and meaning of eschatology. Early in the century Albert Schweitzer's work, *The Quest of the Historical Jesus* (1906), together with Karl Barth's Romans commentary (1918), started the process of rebuilding theology on the foundations of eschatology. Barth put it bluntly: "Christianity that is not entirely and altogether eschatology has entirely and altogether nothing to do with Christ."[1] Schweitzer found himself in the odd position of saying that while the roots of primitive Christianity were embedded in the soil of eschatology, they cannot be transplanted into modern soil. As someone said, Schweitzer did not belong to his own school of thought. Convinced that eschatology was a liability in the effort to modernize Christianity, leading schools of nineteenth-century theology tried to remove its core elements from the presentation of the Christian faith. The "last things" of traditional dogmatics were simply lopped off in favor of various metaphysical, psychological, or ethical reinterpretations of Christianity.

Schweitzer and Barth had the combined impact of shutting the door to a non-eschatological version of Christianity. However, the feeling remained strong that contemporary people can no longer share the eschatological beliefs of the first Christians. Rudolf Bultmann

---

1. Karl Barth, *The Epistle to the Romans*, trans. Edwyn C. Hoskyns (Oxford: Oxford University Press, 1933), p. 314.

made an earnest effort to lay claim to the eschatological heritage of primitive Christianity but reinterpreted its language to fit the categories of existentialist philosophy. The futurist images and beliefs that the early Christians inherited from Jewish apocalypticism were classified as mythical, and thus as so much husk that the winds of time have swept away.

This volume of essays represents a different approach, one that takes seriously the renewal of biblical eschatology and its significance for the faith and theology of the contemporary church. The doctrine of the "last things" has to do with the final future of history and the world; it consists of images of the end of the world, the return of Christ, the resurrection of the dead, and the final judgment. These ideas cry out for fresh interpretation to help believers "give reasons for the hope that is in them." The idea of the eschaton as still future and thus an object of hope is essential to the meaning of eschatology. It is also essential to the renewal of Christian faith and its mission to a postmodern culture lacking a promising image of an authentic future. As a culture we spend a lot of time devising ways to control the future, or even to flee from it.

The biblical-Christian vision of "the last things" makes us citizens of two worlds. There is this world order, this epoch or aeon, St. Paul says, and then there is the coming world, the new age which God is to establish by his power. We can anticipate a future other than what is already present here and now; we call it the kingdom of God or eternal life, and for us it is more real than anything we now experience. In the power of this vision Christians are called and equipped to protest and fight against whatever opposes the coming of God's rule and kingdom.

The "people of God" — Jews and Christians — have received the word of God's promise that this world will be transformed under the impact of the Messiah's coming and the rule of his kingdom. Christianity inherited from Israel most of its own answer to the problems of evil in the world, human sinfulness, and bondage to death. But it offered one amendment to Jewish eschatology, declaring that the promise of the future which Israel kept alive in her traditions is already manifest in the person of Jesus, the Messiah of God. Still there remained a future aspect to be fulfilled at the end of history, when the kingdom of Christ will be handed over to the Father.

The essays in this book indicate that eschatology has somehow been the source of major differences in the history of Christianity, and may still account for many of its major fault lines. They show that profoundly different interpretations of eschatology account for tensions not only between Protestants and Catholics, and between Catholics and Orthodox, but also between the main types of Protestantism. This volume will contribute to a better understanding of these differences, and indicate ways to overcome them.

Carl E. Braaten
Robert W. Jenson

The Task of Christian Eschatology

WOLFHART PANNENBERG

Contemporary Christian doctrine has to live up to an inevitable conflict not with human reason, but with the mentality of our increasingly secularist culture. The truth of Christian doctrine cannot be maintained where Christian proclamation gives priority to adaptation to the secular mentality. It has to challenge that mentality and its prejudices. Of course, Christian doctrine is related to the predicament of human life in our world. Since secularism produces meaninglessness, the human person suffers from the lack of meaning. There is a need, then, for the Christian message, perhaps more urgently so than in other periods of human history. But the message can reach its addressee only if the prejudices of secularism against Christianity can be overcome.

This applies especially to the Christian eschatological hope for a life beyond death. This hope is sharply opposed to the emphatic wordliness of our secular culture. It is under suspicion of escapism, as if it would cheat people out of the fulfillment of their lives on this earth. Gratitude for this life is an essential part of the Christian belief in the creation of this world by God. But the secular mentality exaggerates what we may expect from this finite and mortal life. People expect sex to yield a degree of satisfaction and happiness that it cannot grant without genuine love and fidelity. Political order is expected to produce perfect justice and lasting peace without violence or oppression. But our century has seen totalitarian regimes established precisely in the name of these ideas. The measure of peace and justice that can be obtained under given circumstances and within their limitations depends on the awareness that perfect peace and justice cannot be realistically expected in this world. In social life as well as in individual life it is necessary to accept the limitations of our human situation and not to indulge in exaggerated expectations and demands on our friends and others. Sensitive and mature human persons can be expected to accept the inevitable limitations of this finite life, but then they have to believe in a fulfillment of their deepest human aspiration beyond this earthly life. Without such a belief people are left to seek the narcotic effects of work or diversion by amusement, or they live a life without hope. Actually we live a life without hope already when we stupefy our deeper anxieties and our spiritual emptiness by work or amusement, but also where we indulge in unreasonable expectations. It was one of the spokesmen of liberal theology, early in this century, the German theologian Ernst Troeltsch, who coined the slogan that the next world is the power of life in this world.[1] Hope for a life beyond the present world does not betray this present life, but provides the strength required for the acceptance of its limitations and imperfections. It is true that there is also a danger of withdrawal from this life, and such escapism has been effective in certain forms of Christian spirituality. But it does not characterize the authentic forms of Christian eschatological hope, which rather empowers the believer to affirm this present life, notwithstanding its fragility, affirm it in the light of a future consummation and transfiguration the achievement of which is beyond all human effort and potential.

There is, of course, the question whether such a hope beyond death is reasonable and not delusive. Is there a true and trustworthy basis for such hope? Christian theology must not flinch from this question. Nor is it sufficient to answer it by pointing to the authority of the Bible. Certainly, the biblical revelation offers the basis for our Christian hope. But whether this hope is sustainable and may sustain our life cannot be decided by appeal to the formal authority of the biblical word. Fundamentalist insistence on the formal authority of the Bible as word of God is no appropriate substitute for identifying in the Bible the basis of such hope and for giving an account of the reasons for it (1 Peter 3:15).

When we ask for the truth of our eschatological hope, Christian theology does not only have to face the skepticism of the world, but

---

1. E. Troeltsch, *Die Soziallehren der christlichen Gruppen und Kirchen* (1912), p. 279.

also a long history of critical dissolution of the eschatological conceptions exhibited in the Bible. This critical dissolution occurred in the
history of modern biblical exegesis. The biblical expressions of eschatological hope beyond death have been dismissed as dependent on
now obsolete cultural conditions and on a limited knowledge of natural processes. Furthermore, the early Christian expectation of a near
and catastrophic end of this world is said to have been disproved by
the world's continuing existence for two thousand years. Are there
any good reasons, nevertheless, to resist the tendency towards dis-
missing the biblical eschatology?

The starting point must be the insight that the core of eschatological hope, hope beyond death, is faith in God. Faith in the eternal God
encompasses everything that may be presented as object of Christian
hope. Such hope does not come as something additional to faith in
God, and it cannot persist without such faith. Protagonists of a program of demythologizing the biblical message had a point in reducing
the content of Christian hope to faith in God and in considering all
further explication in terms of a life beyond death superfluous. Communion with the eternal is indeed the crucial thing. "If only I have
you, I do not care for anything in heaven or on earth." This is what Luther found in Psalm 73:25, and the person whose life is so exclusively
focused on God may also continue with the same psalm: "My flesh
and my heart may fail, but God is my strength and my portion forever" (Psalm 73:26).

Here, indeed, nothing more is to be said, because communion with
the eternal God entails whatever our eschatological hope may truth-
fully contain. But then, what in fact does it contain? What does communion with the eternal God beyond our death mean in view of our
human life in its finitude and fragility? Christian eschatology has to explicate this, and such an explication is far from being superfluous. Ab-
stention from any specific exposition of a hope beyond death for the individual and of its relation to the social character of human life may
seem to express a pious preference for not intruding into what God
alone can know. But it can also involve a misunderstanding of what
communion with the eternal God is all about. Faith in God is not compatible with nihilism regarding his creatures, because God himself
wants the life of his creatures, the life of his chosen people, of individual members of his chosen people and, beyond that, of all humankind
restored to communion with himself in Jesus Christ. This being so,

however, it is also appropriate that the human creature of this God longs for a life beyond death. Such longing and hunger for life does not indicate immoderate egotism. The will of the Creator justifies this hunger for life, a hunger that is not satisfied by this earthly life and finds no complete satisfaction short of participation in God's eternity.

The hope of the faithful for unending communion with the eternal God by participation in his eternal life needs a twofold explication, first with regard to the individual life of the human person and second with regard to his or her destiny for a life in communion with other human persons, but also in relationship with the world of creation that forms the context of human life. In the course of such an explication it has to be spelled out what is entailed in the hope that the finite, temporally limited existence of human persons is to participate in the eternal life of God himself, and what it means to say that this will happen through Jesus Christ, by participation in his eternal relationship to the Father as Son of this Father. In other words, these are the traditional themes of Christian eschatology: resurrection of the dead, the kingdom of God, final judgment, and the second coming of Jesus Christ. In the case of the resurrection of the dead, the destiny of the individual is at stake, his or her destiny for a life in communion with God beyond death. In the case of the kingdom of God, the social aspect of human life is concerned, a hope for all humankind in communion with God. The subject of a final judgment is related to the issue of how this finite human life in its autonomous existence can possibly persist in the presence of the eternal God without perishing. The point of the Christian expectation of a second coming of Christ, finally, is how we as finite persons can survive in the confrontation with the eternal God, and the answer will be that this is possible only by participation in the relationship of the eternal and incarnate Son with the Father. All these particular issues are partial aspects of a single issue, i.e., of the participation in the everlasting life of the eternal God by communion with him beyond our finite existence, which is now alienated from God and his eternal glory but shall be transformed into participation of his eternal life without losing its own finite identity.

When we now turn to the particularities of those different aspects of the Christian eschatological hope, the unity of that hope — as emphasized here — recedes in the background. Only in the end, after working through the different particularities of the eschatological sub-themes, can their intrinsic unity be grasped. This result, however, will be the test of whether the individual issues did receive appropriate treatment, because in that case they must convene in the unity of God's communion with his creatures.

Now each particular aspect of the Christian eschatological hope is involved with problems of its own. In the case of the first two issues, the hope for a resurrection of the dead and the hope for the kingdom of God, there is a problem they have in common. It concerns the relationship between anthropology and eschatological hope. Karl Rahner affirmed that there exists a positive relationship between the two, the hope for resurrection corresponding to the individual and the hope for the kingdom of God to the social aspect of human life. On the other hand, eschatological hope can only be based upon God, not on human nature. Therefore, Jürgen Moltmann considered God's promise the only reason for eschatological hope. But God's promise is not opposed to the reality of the human creature. It stands in opposition to human suffering and injustice, but not to the natural aspirations of human beings for some ultimate completion of their lives. Otherwise God's eschatological future and what that entails for God's creatures could not be conceived in terms of promise and hope. The application of terms like "promise" and "hope" presupposes some positive correspondence of the future to come to the present reality of our lives. Therefore, theology should not treat the emphasis on God's promise, which gives reason for our hope, as if it were an alternative to the assumption of an anthropological basis of such hope. It is true enough that only God can bring about the ultimate completion of our human life, but it is also true that human nature is destined from its creation to a fulfillment of its life in communion with its Creator and in a communion of human persons in the kingdom of God.

The kingdom of God is the perfect realization of the destiny of human persons for a life in perfect communion among themselves. Such a communal life is conditioned by peace and justice, because the disruption of peace destroys the community; the preservation of peace, however, presupposes a condition of mutual acknowledgment and acceptance of each other's personality to the effect that each person contributes to the life of the community and receives according to his or her particular status. Unfortunately, the realization of justice in human societies is always disputed and imperfect, and consequently peace remains fragile. There is no situation on earth where all legitimate individual claims are satisfied. Each order of law requires a form of government to be enforced, but even an administration that is empowered by good will cannot always avoid one-sidedness and harshness in individual cases. People contend for their justice against each other, and there is no end of such quarreling in this world. Therefore, prophets like Micah or Isaiah presented their contemporaries with a vision of a future when all nations on earth will assemble at Mount Zion in order to have their quarrels about rights be settled by the God of Israel acting as their arbiter so that they may enjoy everlasting peace thereafter. Thus only the kingdom of God himself will establish genuine justice and consequently permanent peace. By comparison, all human efforts in the service of justice and peace remain provisional. They are necessary and important, nevertheless, but at least Christians should not succumb to the illusion as if an ultimate order of peace among human beings and their nations could be produced by human efforts and especially without regard to either God or religion. Biblical hope tells us to the contrary that only on the basis of faith in the one God will ultimate justice and permanent peace among human beings be obtained. Everything else remains an approximation, a human emergency, and the more soberly people remain aware of this condition, the better the prospect for the relative duration of an always fragile status of human justice and peace on this earth.

Consider what the phrase "kingdom of God" according to the prophetic tradition meant — the replacement of all human forms of government by a human society united by faith in the one God. It becomes clear, then, that the kingdom of God cannot possibly be established by human action aimed at that goal. Neither is the kingdom of God to be conceived as a human empire founded on the Christian faith, nor is it to be realized by the universal mission of the church. The kingdom of God stands in contrast to every worldly state of affairs, which is always marked by compromise. Hope for the kingdom may inspire and direct our human efforts in this world, but its achievement is for another world and puts an end to our antagonistic history of human action. Its advent is the prayer of Christians and Jews alike, though the Christian congregation celebrates its anticipation that already occurred in the mission and history of Jesus.

The idea of an end of our human history connects the hope for the kingdom of God to come with the expectation of the resurrection of the dead. This last one is quite evidently a hope beyond this earthly life, though like the hope for the kingdom of God it does not aim at another life altogether, but rather at the consummation and transfiguration of this our life on earth.

Hope in the resurrection concerns the future of the individual beyond the hour of death. It does so in terms of our communion with the eternal God that does not end in our death.

There are many obvious difficulties that beset the conception of a resurrection of the dead, and they seem almost insurmountable. Christian apologetics had to address them from its beginnings. There is the experiential fact that corpses decay: How, then, can the same body rise again to a new life after a shorter or longer period? And even so, how can it be the same person in view of the interruption of his or her life by death and decay? This second question was answered in Christian theology since the second century by adaptation of the Platonic doctrine of the soul's immortality. The soul was thought to constitute the continuity and identity of individual existence beyond death, though it gets separated from the body in the moment of death, and it receives a new body at the time of the second coming of Christ. In this Christian doctrine the Platonic concept of an immortal soul was considerably modified, because the soul was no longer conceived as migrating through a series of reincarnations as in Plato, but as an element of the individual human person that consists of body and soul, an element that is not the entire human person so that the eternal beatitude of that person requires a reunification with his or her body, which happens in the event of the resurrection. This has been the anthropological defense of the Christian belief in the resurrection since the apologist Athenagoras expounded it in the second century. It was first in Christian theology, of course, that immortality of the soul came to mean participation of the individual human person, with his or her unique life history between birth and death, in God's eternity, quite different from the Platonic soul that transmigrates through a succession of individual lives in the flesh as through a series of changing clothes. Christian hope always related to the concrete individual in his or her unique and unrepeatable life history. This individual is to receive participation in God's eternal life. That distinguishes the Christian hope for individual resurrection from most rival images of an eschatological consummation of this human life on earth.

There remain, of course, deep difficulties with regard to even the conceivability of such a hope, not to speak of the concrete possibility of such an event to occur. The conceptual difficulties can be solved, it seems to me, only on one condition: the assumption that our life, whose history ends in the moment of death, passes away in that moment from our experience, but not from the eternal presence of God. In God's memory our individual life is preserved. Thus, there is no element of our earthly existence that would escape death in order to guarantee our continuous existence beyond death, but only God himself is able, because of his unlimited power, to preserve our temporal lives in his memory and to grant them a new form of existence of their own. It is only from this point of view that the difficulties can be overcome that otherwise prevent the possibility of even imagining a continuous identity of our existence beyond our death. That such a continuous identity does not require the preservation of the material elements of our bodies, was realized as early as Thomas Aquinas. Thomas argued that the material elements of our body are continuously exchanged even in the course of this earthly life. Therefore, our personal identity cannot depend on those material elements, but only on the scheme of our body's reproduction that is located in our soul. Today Christian theology may go one step further. Our personal identity is bound up with the unique and unexchangeable history of our individual life, and that is preserved in the event of our death only in God, even more so than it could be preserved in the memory of a soul that would survive the death of the body.

There are two more specific issues that have to be dealt with in this connection, first the interrelatedness of resurrection and judgment and second the location of the general resurrection at the end of the world's history. Many other issues have to be passed over in silence within the limits of this paper.

In early Jewish tradition, the connection between the expectation of a future resurrection of the dead and the last judgment was that a resurrection of the dead was considered to be presupposed, if dead persons are to receive their divine judgment after their death. In Isaiah 26:14 and 19 and in the New Testament we have a different idea of resurrection. Here, resurrection as such means salvation. In Jesus' word (Mark 12:26f.) as well as in Paul resurrection already imports eternal life in communion with God. But here, resurrection itself involves a transformation, which was otherwise considered a consequence of the divine judgment a person receives, a transformation, that is, either to the better or to the worse. In the words of Paul on the future, the believer's resurrection and transformation are conceived as a single process, a single event (1 Cor. 15:50ff.). Doesn't that mean that resurrection and judgment, which need not involve eternal damnation, belong more closely together than it has been realized in most traditional treatments of these issues? Paul compared the future judgment according to our actions (2 Cor. 5:10) to a great fire which destroys everything that cannot possibly persist in the presence of God. The fire also functions as purification of the more valuable materials used in the building of the church (1 Cor. 3:13-15). If one considers that the transformation of the faithful in the resurrection of the dead is described as transformation into the light of God's glory, does that not suggest a conception of the light of glory and the purifying fire of judgment that burns away everything in our lives that is not compatible with the presence of the eternal God in terms of one and the same reality? In the presence of the eternal God our finite life, which develops in a climate of alienation from God, cannot persist without being transformed. However, some human beings long for such a transformation even now in the course of their earthly life and anticipate it by penitence while others abhor such a transformation as if they suspect it to threaten them with annihilation.

Seen in such a perspective, the separation that occurs in the act of judgment — the separation between what is accepted and what is rejected — loses much of its appearance of relentless and repugnant severity that condemns certain people to eternal punishment. The separation between good and evil remains, since such a separation is the essence of judgment. But it is a separation that applies to each one of us. Each person is to be purified from everything that is incompatible with God's eternal life, though the extent of such purification may be different in each individual case. This point of view has the additional advantage of avoiding the seemingly attractive, but actually cheap alternative of universal reconciliation which would entail the acceptance not only of the sinner, but of evil itself. Evil must be overcome, not accepted. Therefore, judgment is necessary, and according to Paul it will apply to everybody (2 Cor. 5:10), but those united to Christ by faith will be saved even if their works are burned away (1 Cor. 3:15). Will there be other persons of whom the purifying fire will leave nothing? Many biblical words suggest this, though more in the sense of a warning or threat against those who feel secure in their alienation from God. The last judgment must be left to God himself, who created every human person after the image of his Son and who would cer-

tainly seek to recognize some trait of this original design in each one
of his creatures.

Rather than encroach upon God's privilege in a final judgment, it
is important to emphasize that judgment in the sense of purification
applies to all, to each one in the appropriate way, and above all that
this purification indicates at the same time our transformation into
the divine light of glory. Thus the saving dynamic of our resurrection
from the dead is effective in the transformation of our earthly life into
the eschatological life of the "new man," the new humanity, which became apparent first in Jesus' resurrection. This issue of transformation will prove important also in connection with the task of interpreting the Christian hope for the second coming of Christ. Since both are
connected with the assumption of an end of this present world, however, it seems appropriate to comment first on this issue.

In the 1920s it became fashionable to speak condescendingly on
the assumption of an end of this world as it occurs in the biblical writings. The point of Jesus' proclamation of the kingdom of God was focused upon some rare words that point to its present irruption among
those who responded to his message by faith (Luke 11:20). According
to the Gospel of John, the final judgment, too, occurs already (John
12:31) in the confrontation with the word of Jesus (12:48). This exis-
tential concentration of salvation as well as judgment on the present
response to the word felt like a liberation from the traditional Christian worldview and its difficulties with regard to the assumption of a
near end of this world. One of the early protagonists of such a revision-
ist eschatology, however, Paul Althaus, who had published in 1922 a
book on "the last things" that was considered for decades the authoritative treatment of these issues, changed his mind later and revised his
earlier criticism of the eschatological teachings concerning an end of
this world. Why was that considered necessary?

Without the connection of the Christian eschatological hope with
the assumption of an end of the present world, the correlation between the expected future of the individual and that of humankind at
large would be lost. This is the point also in the recent discussion on
whether the resurrection of the individual person happens in the moment of his or her death. Although the individual person enters into
eternity in that moment and the future resurrection of the dead is also
concerned with their transformation into eternal life, still that future
is related to the end of history so that it occurs to all the dead persons

together. In that way, the ultimate future of the individual is connected with that of all humanity. The fact that according to the Christian Easter message, Jesus' resurrection occurred earlier, in the midst of a still incomplete history of humankind, does not contradict the localization of the general resurrection at the end of history, but presupposes it. For the Easter message affirms that in the case of Jesus a reality occurred that is still future to the rest of us, so that Jesus is called "the first born from the dead" (Col. 1:18; cf. 1 Cor. 15:20).

The interconnection between individual and general eschatology by the idea of an end of the present world also applies to the expectation of the kingdom of God. It is only because the full advent of the kingdom of God occurs together with the general resurrection of the dead, that all individual members of humankind will have a chance to participate in the final consummation of human destiny in the kingdom of God. This distinguishes the Christian hope from secularized versions of the hope for the kingdom like Marxism. According to Marxism only future generations of human beings will enjoy the benefits of a classless society, while on the way towards that goal the individuals get sacrificed in its service. By contrast, Christian eschatology unites the future destiny of humankind to that of the individuals of all generations. Thereby, its vision of the end of history overcomes the conflict between the interest of the individuals and that of human society.

Furthermore, in assuming an end of the present world Christian eschatology integrates all of creation into its conception of the final destiny and completion of humankind. A general resurrection of the dead as well as the kingdom of God in this world require a new heaven and a new earth. Not only the finite lives of the human individuals need a profound transformation in order to persist in the presence of God, but the natural conditions of human life, indeed the entire world of nature, need such a transformation (Rom. 8:19-22). This comprehensive implication of the Christian hope corresponds to the fact that it is directed to the God who is the creator of everything. Communion with this God does not admit of an egotistic limitation of hope beyond death to the future of the human individual. It must include the final future of all creation.

The comprehensive vision of a transformation of all things in the light of God's glory can serve, among other things, as a clue to the specific character of art in the context of a Christian culture. It is the transfiguration of present reality, a transfiguration that includes the element of judgment as well as glorification. In the greatest works of Christian artists in the history of Christian culture such a transfiguration of present reality was achieved and thus intimations were presented of the Christian eschatological hope.

In the first half of the twentieth century, however, there seemed to exist a hopeless contradiction between the Christian eschatological hope as related to the assumption of an end of this world and, on the other hand, the worldview of natural science. This probably was a decisive factor in the attempt of some theologians to reduce eschatology to the present experience of faith. But sometimes it is necessary in theology to endure a period of tension in its relationship to the knowledge of the world rather than to adapt prematurely to each new turn in the development of science or even in mere intellectual fashion. In the present situation, tensions seem to relax in the relationship with natural science. Among the sometimes rather speculative models of cosmic development in contemporary scientific cosmology there is a variation that seems surprisingly close to the old Christian expectation of an end of this world combined with a general resurrection of the dead. The cosmological model of Frank Tipler in his "physics of immortality" (1994) may be met with more or less skeptical reserve. It indicates, nevertheless, a new and unexpected openness in the confrontation between scientific cosmology and Christian eschatology, an openness that involves new challenges, but also new opportunities for theology.

The argument of this paper began with the affirmation that faithful trust in the eternal God and the firm communion with him even in the face of death forms the core of all eschatological hope for Christians. If a human person enjoys genuine communion with the eternal God, then even death cannot put an the end to it. Communion with God beyond death does not entail, however, the absorption of our finite existence into the infinite ocean of the divine life. The Creator of the world is determined to affirm the existence of his creatures in distinction from his own, and he sticks to that determination to the very end. That is the confidence of Christian eschatology. The creature, however, cannot persist in the presence of the eternal God except when it acknowledges the sovereignty of God over against one's finitude. The subordination of the Son to the Father, which assumed human concreteness in the relationship of the Davidic king to the God of Israel and later on in the relationship of the people as such to that God, and finally in the incarnation of the eternal Son in Jesus Christ, presents the model of how a creature can enjoy communion with the eternal God. Thus human beings can live in communion with God even beyond their death, when they participate in the relationship of Jesus to God, his heavenly Father. This is the reason why the expectation of a second coming of Christ is inseparable from the other issues of Christian eschatological hope. According to Paul the faithful will go to heaven in order to meet the returning Christ and will "always be with the Lord" (1 Thess. 4:17). His descent from heaven and the resurrection of the faithful form one single chain of events. Accordingly it is said in 1 Corinthians that we shall carry the "image" of the second Adam, we shall rise to a human life penetrated and changed by the origin of all life, the Spirit of God (1 Cor. 15:49), and according to Philippians 3:21 we shall be assimilated to the glorious body of the risen Lord by participation in him. In this way the return of Jesus Christ will inaugurate the consummation of the history of salvation, the communion of a renewed humanity in the kingdom of God, the members of which are united with the eternal God and hence among themselves by participation in the communion of the Son with the Father.

The Recovery of Apocalyptic Imagination

CARL E. BRAATEN

Introduction

"Let anyone who has an ear listen to what the Spirit is saying to the churches" (Rev. 2:7). And what *is* the Spirit saying to the churches of America today? To the church in Ephesus, the message was: "You have abandoned the love you had at first. Remember then from what you have fallen; repent, and do the works you did at first." To the church in Sardis the message was: "I know your works; you have a name of being alive, but you are dead. Wake up, and strengthen what remains and is on the point of death, for I have not found your works perfect in the sight of my God." To the church in Laodicea the message was: "I know your works; you are neither hot nor cold. I wish that you were either cold or hot. So, because you are lukewarm, and neither cold nor hot, I am about to spit you out of my mouth. For you say, 'I am rich, I have prospered, and I need nothing.' You do not realize that you are wretched, pitiable, poor, blind, and naked."

Let those who have ears to hear listen to what the Spirit is saying to the churches of today. As a theologian — and occasionally as a preacher — I have often pondered, "Why, just why, are we so hard of hearing? Why is it so difficult for us to hear what the Spirit is saying to the churches?" This essay is an attempt to answer these questions.

I. The Recovery of Apocalyptic Imagination

I believe we have lost the ability to discern the spiritual dimensions of the warfare in which we are engaged. To put it another way, we have largely lost the apocalyptic imagination to understand the language of the Spirit — to fix our "minds on the things that are above" (Col. 3:2). The apostle Paul called it "discerning the spirits," realizing that "we are not contending against [mere] flesh and blood, but against the principalities, against the powers, against the world rulers of this present darkness, against the spiritual hosts of wickedness in the heavenly places" (Eph. 6:12). Without spiritual discernment we are unable to comprehend the magnitude and the subtleties of the cosmic struggle being fought out on planet earth. And though we say we are Christians and believe in Christ, without the apocalyptic worldview and cosmic framework, we lose sight of what Christ is for. "The Son of God was revealed for this purpose, to destroy the works of the devil" (1 John 3:8). That is not an everyday newspaper sort of language, but an expression of apocalyptic imagination that touches a deeper level of reality.

We all know, of course, that the term "apocalyptic" is notoriously difficult to define, and scholars often accuse each other of using the term in fuzzy ways. The reason is that apocalyptic is both a genre of literature and an entire worldview — a *Weltanschauung* — a many-faceted thing, and not subject to a simple one-line definition. Vaguely we sense it has something to do with eschatology — another conspicuously imprecise word. It includes the idea of the inbreaking of the kingdom from the future, or interpreting history from the perspective of the endtime. The word "apocalypse" simply means "revelation," and is often used to denote the disclosure of final mysteries and meanings hidden from ordinary eyes. Only those to whom the Spirit of God has given eyes to see and ears to hear can grasp "the things which are above." As for the rest, apocalyptic will most likely be dismissed as a pile of hooey, so much dreamlike poppycock having nothing to do with historical events and realities of human experience. Apocalyptic has gotten a bad reputation in part because those most enchanted by this sort of literature mistakenly regard the visions of Enoch or John as providing accurate information about a world above the sky or as reliable forecasts of events piling up at the end of the world.

When Jesus said, "My kingdom is not of this world," he made a revolutionary statement that has had political repercussions down through the centuries. The early Christians caught its meaning in their simple confession, "Jesus is Lord," a confession that prompted Martin Niemoeller to preach in Berlin in the face of the Nazis that only Jesus is our Führer, and no one else — a subversive political statement that got him thrown into jail.

The apocalyptic message is given to communities whose social and cultural worlds are collapsing. The time is ripe and the need is great to recover the apocalyptic imagination in order to strengthen our backbone and stiffen our Christian resistance in face of the rapid moral decline and cultural decay that our society is undergoing. Our schools are not secure, our streets are not safe, our homes with their barred windows look like jails, families are disintegrating, and many churches have exchanged the Word and Sacraments for "bread and circuses."

The apocalyptic perspective does not encourage a wishy-washy attitude on the difference between right and wrong, good and evil, truth and lies, facts and fiction. We need to put back into our speech and outlook concepts like total change, the demonic, signs of the times, conversion, unconditional love of God and neighbor, the reversal of roles, birth pangs of the future, etc. We don't have time to explicate the total worldview of which these are among its core constitutive principles.

John J. Collins concludes his scholarly book on Jewish apocalyptic literature, *The Apocalyptic Imagination*, with these words:

> The apocalyptic revolution is a revolution of the imagination. It entails a challenge to view the world in a way that is radically different from the common perception. The revolutionary potential of such imagination should not be underestimated, as it can foster dissatisfaction with the present and generate visions of what might be. The legacy of the apocalypses includes a powerful rhetoric for denouncing the deficiencies of this world. It also includes the conviction that the world as now constituted is not the end. Most of all, it entails an appreciation of the great resource that lies in the human imagination to construct a symbolic world where the integrity of values can be maintained in the face of social and political powerlessness and even of the threat of death.[1]

1. John J. Collins, *The Apocalyptic Imagination: An Introduction to Jewish Apocalyptic Literature,* 2nd ed. (Grand Rapids: Eerdmans, 1998), p. 283.

Good preaching and theology call for the imagination to go back and forth between the symbols, concepts, and worldview of the Bible, on the one hand, and the ordinary language of our secular world, on the other. The language of the media offers a highly developed vocabulary for speaking about the crushing evils and catastrophes of our day — racism, oppression, violence, terrorism, hunger, homelessness, nuclear annihilation, global warming, overpopulation, environmental poisoning, etc. In contrast, biblical apocalyptic speaks about the powers behind the scenes — Satan, demons, angels good and bad, principalities, dominions, thrones, elemental spirits of the universe, the Dragon and the beasts. Its fundamental story line is the cosmic struggle between the Lord and Creator Spirit of life and "the prince of demons," "the ruler of this world" of death, darkness, and destructiveness. In this worldview, apart from the Devil, the works of God would be diminished; there would be no need of divine redemption, no need of Christ. *Nullus diabolus, nullus redemptor.* Without the Devil and his dominion the biblical story becomes flattened out and one-dimensional, leaving us with "I'm O.K — You're O.K." and other gooey stuff like that. God the redeemer loses much of his identity through the abolition of his opposition, his Satanic antithesis.

The one-dimensional mindset of modernity has tried to do away with the dualistic features of biblical cosmology. Angels, spirits, principalities, powers, demons, and the like supposedly simply do not exist. Or, if we somehow feel bound to concede their existence out of pious deference to the combined weight of Scripture and tradition, we tend to think of them as weightless entities that flit about in the air, and occasionally invade human space from the outside. Not so in the world of apocalyptic thinking. J. Louis Martyn writes: "The dicta most basic to the apocalyptic thinker are these: God created both heaven and earth. There are dramas taking place both on the heavenly stage and on the earthly stage. Yet these dramas are not really two, but rather one drama. . . . The developments in the drama on its heavenly stage determine the developments on the earthly stage. . . . Events seen on the earthly stage are entirely enigmatic to one who sees only the earthly stage."[2] What is really going on is happening on two levels — the heavenly and earthly levels of reality are interconnected. The

---

2. J. Louis Martyn, *History and Theology in the Fourth Gospel* (Nashville: Abingdon Press, 1979), pp. 135-136.

spiritual and material realms are entwined in the biblical drama of salvation, reaching its climax in the story of Jesus and his redemptive victory over Sin, Death, and the Devil.

Modern biblical scholarship has grudgingly conceded the role and significance of apocalypticism in early Christian theology — grudgingly, I say, because at the same time it has devised various demythologizing schemes to neutralize whatever scandalizes the modern mind, in particular any belief in miracles and the reality of demons in this most demonic of centuries. Theologians have been reluctant to accept the full weight of Albert Schweitzer's discovery of the apocalyptic structure and contents of Jesus' eschatology, because that would make him all the more a stranger to modern culture — which, of course, is just the point we should want to emphasize. Henry Cadbury long ago wrote a book entitled *The Peril of Modernizing Jesus*. All this apocalyptic stuff that does not fit our picture of the world can be dismissed as so much mythological husk that can be blown away. So instead we cradle Jesus and his message in the categories of our favorite psychological and sociological theories, as do the scholars of the Jesus Seminar. It was Ernst Käsemann, New Testament theologian of Tübingen, who pronounced in the face of modern demythologizing and existentialist interpretation: "Apocalyptic was the mother of all Christian theology."[3] Käsemann realized that he was taking up one of the forbidden topics in the theology of the academic establishment. He wrote: "Primitive Christian apocalyptic is generally regarded by theological scholars as not being a suitable topic for our day."[4] Pointing a finger at the church he observed that apocalyptic has "seldom enjoyed the goodwill of the dominant church and its theology."[5]

Twentieth-century literature offers some splendid examples of apocalyptic retrieval. C. S. Lewis is most true to the biblical tradition. Not only in *The Screwtape Letters* but also in *Perelandra* the Oxford don depicts a war between good and evil linked to all our individual choices, which have cosmic implications. The material world we see is not the only world there is; hidden within it is a real world of ultimate truths and values that cannot be seen with ordinary eyes, or by reason

---

3. Ernst Käsemann, "The Beginnings of Christian Theology," *New Testament Questions of Today* (Philadelphia: Fortress Press, 1969), pp. 82-107.

4. Ernst Käsemann, "On the Topic of Primitive Christian Apocalyptic," *New Testament Questions of Today*, p. 109.

5. Käsemann, "On the Topic of Primitive Christian Apocalyptic," p. 109.

alone, but only with that sixth sense of spiritual discernment, by faith alone. God and the Devil are both real; it is a materialist delusion to think they do not exist.

Another literary giant is Georges Bernanos, who was part of the Catholic Renaissance in France, along with people like Paul Claudel, François Mauriac, and Antoine Peguy. For Bernanos, as for Lewis, the struggle between good and evil in the individual soul is the microcosm of the cosmic opposition between God and the Devil. There is a void in all of humanity, like unto nothingness, "exuding hatred of God and love of death. Deadly sin lies in associating ourselves with this nothingness, with a 'conscious complicity in Satan's ruses, a lucid acceptance of his power to corrupt and a willingness to come to terms with him.'"[6] His novels picture Satan as the personality at the heart of evil and Christ as the personality at the heart of good. "Without belief in Satan, he argued, one cannot fully believe in God. The world is riddled with evil, and deliberate blindness to that fact obscures the truth about the world and therefore the truth about God. The scale of evil in the world far transcends what humanity could cause itself, and all efforts to improve the world without understanding this transcendence are doomed to failure."[7]

German Protestant theology, from Albrecht Ritschl to Rudolf Bultmann, purged the New Testament of its apocalyptic features, by translating its language into either ethical or existentialist categories. Julius Kaftan, a dogmatician of the Ritschlian School, spoke for many in saying: "If the Kingdom of God is an eschatological matter, then it is useless so far as Christian dogmatics is concerned."[8] Bultmann retained the language of eschatology but radically modified it so as to lose its distinctive apocalyptic content. It was Wolfhart Pannenberg who opened the door to the thought forms of biblical apocalypticism and made good their potential for systematic theology today. The master key for Pannenberg was the notion that the meaning of history cannot be found in the depths of present religious experience but only

---

6. Jeffrey Burton Russell, *Mephistopheles: The Devil in the Modern World* (Ithaca, N.Y.: Cornell University Press, 1986), p. 276. The quote within the quote is from J. E. Cooke, *Georges Bernanos* (Amersham, 1981), p. 33.

7. Russell, *Mephistopheles,* p. 277.

8. Quoted from Rudolf Bultmann's "Foreword" to the English translation of Johannes Weiss, *Jesus' Proclamation of the Kingdom of God* (Philadelphia: Fortress Press, 1971), p. xi.

through a divine revelation of the future end and fulfillment of the whole of history. The death and resurrection of Jesus, apocalyptically interpreted, form the core of the gospel as the present sign of God's future glory and triumph over sin, death, and the power of Satan.

Features of apocalyptic thought relevant to systematic theology are its cosmic dualism, its universal-historical framework, and the expectation of the future end of the world. Hammering these components flat on the anvil of metaphysical monism and a futureless mysticism, the kind of thinking that prevails in "new age" spirituality, results in a betrayal of the New Testament gospel.

II. The Apocalyptic Jesus

The source of the literary imagination of writers like C. S. Lewis and Georges Bernanos is biblical apocalypticism. Seeing the world through apocalyptic eyes began and developed with the Jews, especially during the period between the Testaments. There we find that the main focus was on the faithfulness of God, on what God promised to do in the future to redeem Israel through the coming of the Messiah. In the ministry and message of Jesus the focus of the future curves back upon the present, upon Jesus himself. Jesus not only preached a future messianic kingdom to come; rather, in him the kingdom has already arrived. He is the *autobasileia* — the kingdom itself. Jesus did not merely point to the future in the present; instead, he made present the reality of God's future in a concentrated way. So the attitude that a person takes to Jesus determines the final meaning and personal destiny of one's life.

This motif is very important for believers who struggle with all their might and main for the coming of the kingdom of life over the reign of death, knowing they cannot make it come on their own. The conditions of its coming are not subject to our human power. We are not asked to save the world; only God can do that. Meanwhile, the only way to live as Christian disciples is to resist death and the Devil in whatever earthly forms they appear. And we can do so with hope and confidence because paradoxically we can already celebrate the victory of God over the Enemy, the unholy trinity of Sin, Death, and the Devil. In Christ the decisive battle has already been won. Although we are called to continue the struggle for the dignity of life against the defilement of death, the outcome is no longer in doubt. We shall overcome! We are more than conquerors! This is the ground on which we stand, in light of the apocalyptic vision of the triumph of God over evil in this world.

The *Minneapolis Star Tribune* (August 29, 1998) featured a story about the letters W.W.J.D. — "What Would Jesus Do?" — the latest multimillion-dollar bonanza for companies marketing bracelets, T-shirts, pens, key chains, books, calendars, stuffed animals, and tote bags, selling not only in Christian boutiques but in mainstream stores like K-Mart. "What would Jesus do?" sounds like the right question. Right? Wrong! — the wrong question, because it lets us off the hook; it puts us in charge of the answer. The right question is "What *did* Jesus do?" and how does that tell us "Who he *is*"? Christians have always looked to the real Jesus of the Gospels in search of a word, a model, a promise, or a sign, to challenge us, to direct us, to clue us in as to where to stand, when to march, how to act. After all the revolutions in recorded history have come and gone, there remains the revolutionary message and ministry of Jesus that outlasts and transcends them all. He read his first manifesto in the synagogue, taken from the prophet Isaiah:

> The Spirit of the Lord is upon me,
> because he has anointed me to preach good news to the poor.
> He has sent me to proclaim release to the captives
> and recovering of sight to the blind,
> to set at liberty those who are oppressed.

He came to the defense of the defenseless. He took sides in the struggle of life for the poorest of the poor, forgotten people locked up in jails, the blind, all the victims of oppression. It doesn't stretch the imagination too much to include the most helpless of all — abused children and the millions of unborn little ones, treated like garbage for the sake of someone's personal convenience.

Jesus never talked about gradual measures, minor improvements, piecemeal changes, or just a little bit of progress. He had an all-or-nothing way of speaking. He was not for reform, but repentance; not for accommodation but conversion. He did not talk about the happy medium, the middle way, the golden mean. It was the mark of his apocalyptic mindset to speak in absolutes, in total terms, complete transvaluation, involving a reversal of signs so that plus is minus and minus is plus. No wonder the apocalyptic Jesus appears as a stranger to our times.

The call of the kingdom is not to become a little better, but for a radical turning away from the old ways to a new life. In this new life there are deeds to be done. Discipleship calls for discipline, moral clarity, and behavioral consistency. When Jesus through his Spirit brings the rule of his Father into our lives, he first of all brings the love of God, granting forgiveness to the wretched sinners we are. But he was never heard preaching an unconditional love and acceptance that leaves people in their sins — that kind of popular mushy sentimentality blind to the sins marked out for condemnation under the judgment of God.

When the kingdom of God, the rule of God's love, claims a person, one must be prepared to sacrifice whatever gets in the way of our love and loyalty to God. It may be parents, possessions, profession, or patriotism. Extreme measures are called for — an offending eye must be plucked out and an evil-doing hand cut off. One must be prepared to be despised, ridiculed, and ostracized by old friends and esteemed colleagues. A clean-cut choice has got to be made. God and Mammon cannot both be served; either we carry the cross of the kingdom or we seek the security of the system. I know some young aspiring scholars afraid to speak or write on certain forbidden topics, or even to be closely associated with those who do, lest their chances of climbing the academic ladder be jeopardized. "Whoever does not renounce all that he has cannot be my disciple." That is an offensive statement. This unconditional surrender of all your heart and soul and mind to the rule of God's love means this: if you give your whole life away like that, that is the only way really to get a life.

And who knows what can happen when such an apocalyptic reversal of ordinary religion and everyday morality takes place, what new dreams, new thrusts, and new directions may lead to a more just and peaceful society? This gets down to the nitty-gritty of social morality, economic systems, political structures, and juridical procedures. What the Bible calls "principalities and powers," from whose systems of domination Christ has set us free, are the driving determinants behind the backs of these cultural institutions of our day. These "spiritual forces of evil in the heavenly places" are not floating in the air beyond distant clouds; they are rather the spiritual heart and soul of earthly institutions that conspire against life and the Giver of life, the same public institutions that joined forces to pronounce the death penalty and execute the Lord of life on a criminal's cross.

III. Cross and Resurrection: The Turning Point of History

Jesus died a public death in a public place at the hands of public forces. Organized religion put Jesus to death. The economy got involved, graft and greed and bribery in the hands of the moneychangers. Blood money put Jesus to death. The judicial process swung into action — a kangaroo court, a flunky judge, false witnesses, concocted charges; a corrupt juridical system put Jesus to death. And the mob fell in line with the ruling class, chanting idiot slogans to heat up the blood in their veins. They had been programmed to thrive on violence, to sink into sadism, and switch from the hosanna chants of one weekend to the cries of "Crucify him" the next. The polls and public opinion, voices from the conservative cliques, the radical rabble, or the middle-class masses all had a hand in putting Jesus to death. And then there was the military. Soldiers were there to carry out the will of the ruling oligarchy. They stripped him and beat him and pressed thorns into his scalp. They only did what they were ordered to do, trained as they were to do the bidding of Rome. And so they drove the spikes through his hands and feet. They gambled for his clothes. And Jesus was dead, literally dead.

All of that you could have seen with your eyes if you had been there. It was a public affair. But the New Testament sees into the spiritual depths of the cross. It was not just a bad mix-up at city hall, resulting in the unfortunate death of an innocent man. The cross and the resurrection together mark the apocalyptic turning point of history. "On that cross he [God] discarded the cosmic powers and authorities like a garment; he made a public spectacle of them and led them as captives in his triumphal procession" (Col. 2:15 NEB). Luther had a similar knack of seeing what lies beneath the surface plane — what I have called apocalyptic imagination. The cross was a trap God set for the Devil. "The Devil saw Jesus as his prize, snapped at the bait, and was pulled out of the water for all to see."[9] Sin, Death,

---

9. Quoted from Walter Wink, *Engaging the Powers* (Minneapolis: Fortress Press, 1992), p. 140.

and the Devil were the real but hidden powers at play in the passion of our Lord. And that's why the victory of the cross is so great and unique; it deals with the profoundest dimensions of human bondage. Jesus "gave himself for our sins to set us free from the present evil age, according to the will of our God and Father" (Gal. 1:4). Jesus "himself bore our sins in his body on the cross" (1 Peter 2:24). "We speak God's wisdom," Paul writes, "secret and hidden, which God decreed before the ages for our glory. None of the rulers of this age understood this; for if they had, they would not have crucified the Lord of glory" (1 Cor. 2:7-8). It took a good dose of spiritual discernment, of apocalyptic imagination, for Paul to view Christ's death as salvation from the wrath of God (Rom. 5:9), or to see Christ as a paschal lamb sacrificed on our behalf.

The death of Christ was interpreted by Paul in light of the resurrection as an eschatological event at the outer edge of history. Whenever Paul said anything about the resurrection of Jesus, he was presupposing the apocalyptic worldview and conceptuality. Thus, the resurrection can only be understood in terms of the expectation of a universal resurrection of the dead, which will coincide with the manifestation of the full and final glory of God. The death and resurrection of Christ mark the incursion of the future age into the old age in which we live. This is intelligible only by understanding the grammar of apocalyptic language.[10]

The church now looks ahead to a future coming of the Christ who has already come in the flesh, because of a contradiction between what it experiences here and now and the promise of eternal life epitomized in the resurrection of Jesus. The power of the new age is already at work in the church, since the Holy Spirit, who is the pledge of the new age, is already present in believers' hearts and in their midst. One of Pannenberg's favorite words is "proleptic," a word that helps us understand the logic of apocalyptic thought. The sacrament of Holy Baptism is a proleptic experience of the new age, new life in the Spirit, made possible through the death and resurrection of Jesus Christ. In our baptism we renounced the Devil and all his works and ways, even though in real life we continue to do business with him. Paul is keen to associate our freedom with baptism, our living through dying with

10. J. Christiaan Beker, *Paul the Apostle: The Triumph of God in Life and Thought* (Philadelphia: Fortress Press, 1980), pp. 135ff.

Christ. "Therefore we have been buried with him by baptism into death, so that, just as Christ was raised from the dead by the glory of the Father, so we too might walk in newness of life. . . . We know that our old self was crucified with him so that the body of sin might be destroyed, and we might no longer be enslaved to sin" (Rom. 6:4, 6). Baptism is our entrance into a countercultural community that, instead of cozying up to the powers-that-be, has the courage to tangle with the demonries of our time, to engage the structures of destruction, the rulers and powers in high places.

Christians will always live in a crisis situation between the powers of death and the powers of life. The rulers of this present world order, the old age, have not only crucified Christ but continue to crucify those who belong to Christ. The church is the place in which the new world of God is dawning in the midst of the old, and therefore a place where antagonistic forces battle for the soul of the church.

The Seer of the Apocalypse writes:

"Let anyone who has an ear listen:
If you are to be taken captive, into captivity you go;
if you kill with the sword, with the sword you must be killed.
Here is a call for the endurance and faith of the saints."

The church must be careful about what means it uses to fight the forces of evil. Its only defense is the "shield of faith" and its only weapon is the "sword of the Spirit, which is the word of God" (Eph. 6:16-17). Therefore, Christians must not imagine they can help bring in the kingdom by fighting violence with violence. Even though I have not been a card-carrying pacifist all my life, I have nevertheless admired people like Tolstoi, Gandhi, certain Quakers I have known, and my philosophy teacher and Kierkegaard scholar, Howard Hong, who derived their inspiration from a literal acceptance of the words of Jesus. Jesus spoke in negatives as though to warn us against trying to bring in the kingdom in worldly ways. He spoke as though he did not expect many of us would have the guts to do it his way — the way of suffering and the cross. Perhaps he was expecting at most a tiny cadre of followers, of faithful disciples. So he said in effect: "My little band of followers has got to be different." You must not get angry or swear; you must not be a hypocrite; you must not see the splinter in your brother's eye, and don't brag about your good deeds; don't put a lot of money in the bank. And don't worry about tomorrow; it takes the joy and humor out of today. Don't be greedy and full of spite. If you lose, don't get mad at the guy who beat you. Say, nice going, good shot, not out of pretense and good manners, but from the heart. When you pray, don't show off, using nice pious words and the rote repetition of ritualistic phrases.

Who cares to join the movement headed up by Jesus? He does not make it easy for us. Don't just love your family and friends; love your enemies. It's easy to pray for those who love you back. Try praying for those you oppose, whose deeds you contemn, the people on the other side. And don't seek revenge, but get the hate out of your heart. If someone enjoys hitting you on the cheek or below the belt, let him do it again. Give and expect nothing in return.

IV. The Good News of the Apocalypse

The apocalyptic word and model that came to expression in Jesus is paradoxically the good news. Yet, it is the good news for us living in precarious times. We are discovering that the American church is dying of its own success. It has tried hard to be relevant to its cultural setting, to foster a faith and worship practices that make people feel good. Churches that grow are the ones that seem to satisfy the search for self-fulfillment. They travel light. Churches that have traditionally defined themselves in terms of a core of biblical and confessional doctrines and practices, that retain the catholic substance of the church's tradition, its dogmas, liturgies, hymnody, and moral codes, carry so much baggage that they find it hard to compete with "Christianity Lite." Pastors are pressured to get with it, to quit being hidebound to the traditional ways of being church. They are told to be more user-friendly. The pastor of one megachurch that successfully packs them in by the thousands was asked, "How do you do it?" His answer: "When people come to our church, we want them to leave feeling like they have not even been in church."

We are living in apocalyptic times without an apocalyptic faith and theology. We are trying to use a theology of the establishment and for the establishment to grapple with the life-and-death issues that hang in the balance. In the language of the Apocalypse of John, we must be prepared to name and challenge the actions of the Beast and the

Dragon in our time, in our society, even in our church. We are not fighting against flesh and blood. It's not merely a case of bad politicians who could be replaced by good politicians. We are dealing with structures of worldwide destruction of cosmic proportions, with powers and principalities, with the Dragon and the Beast.

The Apocalypse of John was written at a time when Christians were in grave danger. Rome was beginning to enforce the cult of emperor worship. Some in the church were advocating a policy of compromise. John had a vision and then wrote it down to encourage the faithful to stand fast, to resist the demands of emperor worship, even unto death. Again and again in our century, at times of severe peril and persecution, this book has come back into play. And to think that at one time the Book of Revelation barely made it into the canon of Scripture, and would have been thrown out if some theologians had their way!

Ernst Käsemann — I come back to him from time to time — specified: "For the first time in remembered history the tide is running against us, and for the first time since the early days of Christianity it is possible seriously to imagine that the vision of the Book of Revelation is literally being fulfilled: that the Antichrist is enthroned visibly and universally on the graves of the saints and only in the desert is there room for the people of God."[11]

There are many pastors and theologians who would question the wisdom of reviving the antagonistic rhetoric of apocalyptic: God and Satan, angels and demons, good and evil, heaven and hell, life and death, cross and resurrection. These are not the sorts of things we learn about in the core curriculum of most divinity schools. Moreover, the symbols of the apocalypse have often been made into the speculative playthings of eschatological sharpshooters, gazing into the remote future and concocting unreal agendas of "last things." The point is rather to reappropriate language and images that match the realities of the present.

In Christian history the symbols and images of apocalyptic revelation have provided words of exhortation and consolation that meet the problems of the day, encouragement in the face of persecution, confidence in the face of culture shock, support in the wake of histori-

11. Ernst Käsemann, "Theologians and Laity," *New Testament Questions of Today*, p. 288.

cal disaster, courage in times of helplessness, and comfort in the throes of death.

Apocalyptic symbols help us to see things in light of their antithetical relations. There is no Christ alone simply as such; his identity is established in relation to his opposite, the Antichrist. There is no gospel by itself; it must be spelled out in contrast to the law and judgment of God. The sense of the holy is experienced in contrast to what is profane. In the Gospels it is the demon-possessed who are able to recognize the Christ. The identity and meaning of Christ go hand in hand with the works of the Antichrist. If Christ means freedom and liberation, the politics of the Antichrist means domination, oppression, slavery. The work of Christ exists in direct opposition to the principalities, the world rulers of this present darkness, the spiritual hosts of wickedness (Eph. 6:12).

Reasonable people are invoking the categories of apocalyptic to frame the culture wars being waged in the media, in education, in religion, politics, and in law. Peter Kreeft calls for an "ecumenical jihad" to stand up against the culture wars that are fast eroding the fundamentals of religion, morality, and law on which a good society is based.[12] When abortion and homosexual behavior, things that clearly contradict the commandments of God and two thousand years of Christian teaching, are accepted as merely matters of personal choice and lifestyle preference, we find ourselves up to our noses in the sludge of social decay and decadence. It boggles the mind. Politicians, the majority of them, tolerate laws of leniency in the name of enlightenment; educators en masse endorse them; the media celebrate them. Meanwhile churches are divided; theologians, many of the best of them, have long since slid down the slippery slopes of relativism and pluralism.

The Apocalypse of John pictures imperial Rome in terms of the Dragon and the Beast. Can that picture be superimposed on the American Empire or Western Europe? Are we still contending with the Dragon and the Beast? I don't know, but if the shoe fits. . . . So let us listen to how the Apocalypse depicts the Dragon and the Beast. The Dragon has given colossal power to the Beast; and the Beast sits on the throne and wields great authority. People fear, love, and trust that authority above all things. John was worried that even Christians were

---

12. Peter Kreeft, *Ecumenical Jihad* (San Francisco: Ignatius Press, 1996).

willing to bend their knees. They say the authority is to be trusted because the authority knows best. They say there is no one like the Beast; it is the proudest power — the greatest nation — in the history of the world. It cannot be wrong; it cannot be defeated. Honor and pride belong to the Beast. Who can stand up against it? The mouth of the Beast utters haughty and blasphemous words. The Beast is blaspheming the name of God because it makes war on the saints. The Beast is a world imperialist; it exercises authority over every tribe and people and tongue and nation. It dominates the world's markets; it exports instruments of violence and vice. It sneers at the ways and customs of other people. It succeeds in making its language the *lingua franca* of all nations and continents. And it forces all the little people of the world to live off the crumbs that fall from the table, that trickle down to them from the top. And John says, if you really want to know what's going on, you must know about the Dragon and the Beast, the deeper realities hidden behind the apparent causes and daily headlines. What John found most lamentable was that Christians were confused about what was going on. Someone has said, the church which is to be the searchlight is more often the taillight of every new movement in the world. There were Christians, John saw, who were willing to live a hyphenated existence with the Beast, not satisfied with an exclusively Christian identity but willing to compromise, to accommodate a worldly political affiliation. John feared that Christianity would become an adjective to sanction and support the operations of the Beast in the world. Watch out, you who have been signed with the cross, lest you too bear the mark of the Beast. Christianity becomes an adjective when Christ is not the soul and substance of the church, the sole head of the body. In his *Attack on Christendom* Kierkegaard warned (I am paraphrasing): "Little by little and now at last Christianity has become exactly the opposite of what it is in the New Testament." Of course, they said Kierkegaard was known occasionally to exaggerate.

Conclusion

So what to do? How can you fight the Beast when, if you get rid of one, the Dragon will dispatch another? The first thing, John said, is to remain faithful, and the second is to remember you're in the struggle for the long haul, until the day Christ returns in all his glory. So what are the people of the endtime to do in the meantime? What does it mean to remain faithful?

We are followers of the Lamb that was slain. Brawls in the alleys won't do. "If anyone slays with the sword, with the sword must he be slain." The Lamb was slain so that we will slay no more. We are free to die on a cross, but not to place another person's body on the rack. We know there will be violence, for it is sheer stupidity to think that the Beast will be a silent spectator of its own demise and destruction. And here is the good news of the Apocalypse. The gospel tells us that the Dragon has received a mortal wound. We can hardly keep from laughing in the face of the Beast, because we know that the entire imperial network of powers under the authority of the Dragon has more than met its match. There is no longer any reason for gloom and despair. We are buoyed up by the liturgical celebrations of the church and we sing the hymns of victory even now in the midst of the struggle. One of the verses proclaims: "The devil has come down to you with great wrath, because he knows that his time is short" (Rev. 12:12). Worship is the most potent political weapon we have, which is why John had to condemn every form of emperor worship, because it resulted in giving away what is most precious — the gift of freedom to worship God and God alone in purity and in truth. Idolatry is the greatest sin, and blasphemy its next of kin.

In the meantime, eschatologically speaking, the church will always be a resistance movement in the world, resisting evil and the agents of death, resisting the wiles and ways of the Dragon and the Beast. The struggle will never end, and will always have a specific target. But let it not be said we are down in the mouth, for we are born anew to celebrate the victory of God in the midst of apparent setbacks. In the very midst of strife and suffering, we can always sing a hymn, say a prayer, and know that God is with us.

Those who engage in the struggle for life against death, lacking the resources of faith and worship, are often people of courage and virtue, but they can't be trusted to hang in there for the long haul. And that is because Christian ethics does not stand on its own feet; its resource lies in the depths of faith that reaches into the heart of God. Many partners in the struggle look for social change based on humanistic moral guidelines, but they chicken out when the going gets rough. They are likely to respond to political setbacks in moods of resignation and despair. They lack the eschatological perspective embedded in the eucharistic liturgy of the church. For liturgy is basically eschatology, the sacramental communication of God's future under the conditions of these troubled times. In the liturgy we are reminded that even when we lose a battle or two, we are still assured of the outcome.

Here again the Apocalypse can help us. It was Michael and his angels who fought against the Dragon. Good news! We are not in it alone. What defeated the Dragon, "that ancient serpent who is called the Devil and Satan, the deceiver of the whole world" (Rev. 12:7)? Not the number and power of the saints who took him on in hand-to-hand combat. Rather, "they have conquered him by the blood of the Lamb and by the word of their testimony, for they did not cling to life even in the face of death" (Rev. 12:11). Satan is cast down, stripped of his power, and it is only a question of time before he will be thrown into the lake of fire. His eternal fate is sealed; his days in time are numbered.

To understand and make use of such strange language in preaching requires apocalyptic imagination. Only those who have eyes to see can see what the Seer has seen in his vision. The Seer prophesies that when repression is visited upon the saints, the numbers will grow, as has dramatically occurred in China and other Communist countries, proving that the "the blood of the martyrs is the seed of the church." Christians have no right to expect a better hand than the System dealt to their commander in chief — the way of suffering and the cross — a mark of the true and faithful church!

Jesus, the one who was slain by the Dragon and the Beast, who has been exalted to heaven, who now sits at the right hand of the Father, holds the whole world in his hands. This is the victory that supports our faith. The rule of God has already begun. The authority of Christ is not pie in the sky by and by. His will is being done already now on earth as it is in heaven. We may exercise the power of prayer to pray for our enemies; we have been given the gift to make peace in the throes of violence; we have the uncanny ability to love those we otherwise would hate, and we face the prospect of death in the joy of life.

With apocalyptic imagination we hold, contrary to all appearances, and therefore paradoxically, that the Lordship of Christ is already fully established. Our faith in the power of the Spirit is invincible; it cannot deceive us. What we hold in our imagination we declare already as fact on account of Christ.

> Then the seventh angel blew his trumpet, and there were loud voices in heaven, saying,
>
>> "The kingdom of the world has become the kingdom of our Lord and his Messiah, and he will reign forever and ever." (Rev. 11:15)

The Great Transformation

ROBERT W. JENSON

I have dealt with the matter of this essay before, at the end — where else? — of my systematic theology. I will try to repeat myself only a little.

I begin with some presumptions. I will not here argue that Scripture does in fact promise a final goal of God's way with his creation, nor will I argue that this is somehow a comprehensive and thorough transformation of the antecedent state of affairs. Should somebody wish to dispute these presumptions, the dispute would be about biblical hermeneutics, another subject than that assigned for this essay. What God creates is not a timeless cosmos, which thereafter acquires a history. What God creates is a history, which is a creation, a whole, because it is brought to a completion. Just so there *is* a completion, and one that does not just start everything up again. That is, there is what theology has called an "eschaton."

That there is to be a final transformation is established in old Israel's Scripture. Read as narrative, the whole Old Testament looks to the fulfillment of the Lord's promises to Abraham, that his descendants would be God's own people, and that this people would be the means of God's blessing to all peoples. It is possible to construe all the canonically told history of Israel as the Lord's exegesis of these promises.

At the end of canonical Israel's history, in the proclamation of the exilic and post-exilic prophets, the promises are unveiled as eschatological, that is, as unfulfillable under the conditions governing history as we now experience it. These prophets proclaimed the gathering of

33

all humanity to the God of Israel, not merely inwardly but politically and cultically, and the establishment thereby of a universal and eternal community of justice and peace. Such events clearly exceed the possibilities of this world. Moreover, as prophecy achieved its final mode in apocalyptic, the prophets became reflectively explicit that this is so. The fulfillment of the Lord's promises must be the end of the way things go now and the reality of a whole new way for things to go.

The New Testament adds no new content to this. Jesus appears as prophet of the kingdom of God, that is, of just this eschatological fulfillment of the promises to Abraham. What was new about his prophecy was not content but style, the imminence with which the kingdom appeared in his proclamation and action: if canonical Israel's prophets spoke *about* the end of days, Jesus' message and deeds *occupied* that end. Thus — and this is decisive for specifically Christian eschatology — in the presence of Jesus, standing at the doors of the kingdom and following Jesus himself could not be distinguished.

Jesus was then raised from the dead. This event is also God's interpretation of the promise to Abraham. The resulting situation can be laid out as a sort of argument. To follow Jesus is to stand at the kingdom's gate; this was already the case before his death and resurrection. That Jesus is resurrected means that he has entered the kingdom; therefore following him now means following him through that door. But the resurrected Jesus is the one of whom Paul had to say, "He lives in me and I live in him." Therefore entering the kingdom by following Jesus is simultaneously entering into Jesus. And so finally, being on the way through the gate into the kingdom and being one with Christ are the same thing; and being in the kingdom and being perfectly in Christ will be the same thing.

Thus expectation of the Old Testament's fulfillment, of the Grand Transformation of the conditions of being there promised, is not a detachable or optional item of Christian faith. Faith in Jesus and eschatological expectation are but two aspects of one mode of existence. It is a chief disaster of the modern church, at least in its "mainline," that we think we can separate them, that we can believe in Christ without robust eschatological expectation. The folk who drive around with bumper stickers about the Rapture are closer to biblical faith than are most mainline Christians, with our embarrassment about such matters.

Yet there *is* something the matter with those bumper stickers, and modern Christianity's embarrassment is not *only* a lack of faith. How are we to conceive the eschaton? The bumper stickers represent the attempt to construct out of Scripture's apocalyptic passages one authoritative apocalyptic scenario, a "biblical" depiction of the end as a sequence of events that starts at some time in the history of this age and eventuates in the actuality of the kingdom. Scripture indeed sometimes presents the end as such a sequence; we can find in the Bible more than one apocalyptic scenario. But here, I think, we are required to demythologize a bit.

For one thing, the biblical scenarios can only with violence be fitted together into a single coherent scenario, which might then indeed have some biblical authority. For another, the New Testament's scenarios all suppose the chronologically speedy return of Christ, which did not happen. Some churches have in fact *mandated* demythologizing here, by condemning chiliasm, which means condemning the Bible's most detailed scenario.

And finally, there is a more conceptual objection. Each of the usually depicted apocalyptic events, if considered in its character as a fulfillment of the promise, turns out in fact to be a complete fulfillment, requiring no preliminary or further events. When most neo-Protestant theologians insisted that the Transformation had to be conceived as one concluding event, they got something right. At the present moment, Christians are divided on this matter: some are hatching plots to rebuild the Jerusalem Temple, by way of getting the apocalyptic sequence started; others think this misguided. I am with the latter group.

The Messianic Woes, the millennium however located with respect to the return of Christ, the return of Christ itself, the reunion of Judaism and the church, the Resurrection, the Last Judgment, the coming of the New Jerusalem, should all, I think, be construed as aspects of one great event. That is the formal part of the proposal made in this essay.

It does not, however, follow that nothing can be narrated about this event, that there is no eschatological story to tell. What we cannot do is tell a story in which the Resurrection precedes the Last Judgment and the Last Judgment the beatific vision and so forth. That is, what can be told of is the Great Transformation itself, the eternal final event, participation in which is our destiny. We can tell a story of a single event because in its deepest aspect the Great Transformation is our entry into the life of the triune God, who indeed has a story yet is one single God; I will return to that at greater length.

I will here tell of this event under three of the biblical rubrics for it: as the coming of the New Jerusalem, the Last Judgment, and deification. And I will summarize all three under a fourth rubric.

The End Is a Final Polity, the New Jerusalem

The dominant biblical descriptions of the final goal are all political, which is why I start here. What is coming is God's kingdom of Heaven, his new city of Jerusalem. All nations will be gathered by the Messiah, the final anointed king of David's line. Political descriptions of the eschaton do not dominate in Scripture because the biblical writers looked around for the best language with which to evoke the eschaton; they dominate because the biblical story that needs a completion *is* the story of a nation, Israel, and the problems and hopes of its common, that is to say political, life. In an early book, *Story and Promise,* I made it seem as if there were a variety of ways of evoking the eschaton, of which political language was only one, and that the way one chose on an occasion was a matter of context. This was not quite right. There is in fact one sort of biblical eschatological discourse which is foundational for the rest, and that is the political sort.

The great political problem is the problem of the center, and that problem, I maintain, is solved only eschatologically. If a mass of people is to be a community, they must have something in common. And the traditional wisdom of humanity has held that this something can only be a common "good," a joint object of desire, something that draws persons together in loving aspiration.

Now if this good is the universal good, i.e., God, all is well. But then of course the End is come. It is precisely the fact that all nations have *not* come to Zion that determines the conditions of this age. In this age the communal objects of desire can only be partial goods, and just so occasions of conflict between communities or individuals who adhere to different goods. This is true even of Christianity, so long as the church is divided, as it always has been. Constantine once hoped that establishing the church could establish general peace in this world; it would have worked, had the church itself been united, that is, were the church already in the kingdom.

Western modernity is constituted by many factors, but one of them is the determination to avoid conflict over incompatible visions of the common good. Such conflict was horrifically demonstrated to seventeenth-century Europe and its North American extensions by the European wars of religion. Viewing the wreckage, the European and North American elites vowed, "Never again." And to carry out this vow, the modern West embarked upon an unprecedented experiment: of replacing common dedication to the good with machinery for the adjustment of disagreements about the good. The common in community was no longer to be a common good to be achieved, but a common apparatus by which conflicting desires are adjusted.

For a few privileged nations, the mechanization of community has worked quite well. Once Americans got the civil war out of our system, the machinery of representative and bureaucratic democracy has enabled us to live together in very tolerable peace. But as some predicted from the first, the experiment has in the longer term emptied our life together of moral or aesthetic or indeed even emotional substance. For a trivial but telling symptom: within my own lifetime, the great American moral and emotional festivals, where the democratic machinery itself was an object of enthusiasm or even love, have been turned into days at the mall.

In less privileged places, the emptiness of mechanized common life has broken out in such communal despair as to become itself an occasion of violence, indeed of such hatred-fueled violence as to make late modernity the bloodiest of all periods. And in America and Western Europe also, the elites embrace various nihilisms, while the rest endure a common life constituted mostly in relentless manipulation.

Let me draw the facit. Humanity short of the kingdom is divided by precisely the pursuit of a common good that might bind it together. Liberal democracy hoped to avoid this by eschewing that pursuit, but neither has this move solved the political problem. Christians know why: only against the church will the gates of hell not prevail. No polity of this world can in the long run survive its inner contradictions; Marx was right, except in thinking that a proletarian polity would somehow be immune to this law.

The kingdom will be the sheer presence of the triune God to all humanity. As the Revelation evokes it, "[I]ts temple is the Lord God the Almighty and the Lamb. And . . . the glory of God is its light and its lamp is the Lamb." That is, the End will be the utter worship of

God, as our hearts at last find their love in him; and just so, a perfect availability and dedication of each of us to all the rest of us. It will be the *sheer happening* of what the Old Testament calls "righteousness." It will be what all earthly polities seek to bring to pass and do not.

All that is very abstract. To think this explosion of righteousness more actually, we must turn to a different aspect of the Great Transformation, its character as the Last Judgment.

The End Will Be a Last Judgment

Since it is the Bible that proclaims a final judgment, our first task is to remind ourselves of what that book means by judgment. In Scripture, judgment is intervention to restore righteousness, that is, to set a community right. The notion is something like the following. In the community of Israel, or the church, or by extension any community viable for more than a moment, each person occupies a unique position over against all the others, constituted by a specific set of what we would now call rights and duties. Righteousness prevails when each person takes his or her such location as an opportunity of loving service to all the rest. To the extent that such love fails, the community is disordered and *unrighteousness* prevails. Whether it is then a parent intervening in a quarrel between siblings, or a jury and judge determining the facts and the law, or the Lord intervening to judge all Israel, judgment is action to sort out a polity not living in love. So the prosperous landholder in Israel who does not use his prosperity to serve his impoverished neighbors, who, e.g., strips his fields so clean that there are no gleanings, commits injustice, and the town elders must reprove him in the gate and compel him to more communally responsible behavior. And if the created magistrates do not function, eventually God intervenes to save the community from its own lack of love.

The *Last* Judgment is simply a judgment that encompasses the entire human community and after which another will not be needed. It will be the act of God in which all the accumulated injustice of history, of the total human community, is put right, and humanity is made one vast network of unique persons each taking his or her uniqueness as the opportunity of love for all the rest. So a child's disobedience will be set right between him and his parents, and the bombings of Coventry and Dresden between Germany and the Allies, and the eternal mutual oppression and violence of races and classes; and for that matter the hegemony involved in my presuming to write this essay, will all be put right.

Plainly, the last judgment just described is not the last judgment of much apocalyptic imagining, a sorting operation on individuals, to pick them out for heaven or hell. I do not mean to deny that individuals will indeed be judged. The robber baron will be condemned for his exploitation of the helpless, and reparation made. The brutal parent will be rebuked and the harm done the children repaired. And perhaps this will be not be accomplished without excluding some from the blessed community altogether, so that indeed there comes to be a final community of love and another one of hatred, called hell. But that sorting is not the primary reality of what we may await. The primary reality of what we may await is the establishing of universal and perfect justice, which on the biblical understanding of justice is the same as the establishing of universal and perfect love.

This setting right should not be seen as a sort of preliminary, clearing the decks for the establishment of universal bliss. This setting right is itself the *content* of the eternal event of bliss. What happens as final salvation? Precisely *that we are set right* with each other, that I have the *joy of God's rebuke* for my sin against my brothers and sisters, and the joy of seeing the repair of my injuries to them, at my cost. The point is of fundamental importance, for it is just so that it is *me*, in *my* identity as the sinner I am, who lives the joy of the kingdom. The blessed eternity will be as it were the eternal expansion of one great *reconciling*.

Finally on this line, the Last Judgment must be also *our* act of mutual forgiveness and reparation; we must be reconciled with one another.[1] The proposition would be Pelagian, if a final mutual reconciliation were construed as an event prior to entry into the kingdom, and so as a sort of condition of entrance. But my proposal is that reconciliation, including this last aspect, is the life of the kingdom itself.

---

1. I take this point from Miroslav Volf, in conversation and in papers prepared for the Center of Theological Inquiry.

The End Will Be Deification

The metaphysically deepest characterization of the End is as "deification," or what is finally the same thing, beatific vision.

Let me put the question: What *could* be an end of history, other than a sheer and thus meaningless termination? God, we said, creates a history that is a whole, a creation, only because it has an end. But what could "an end" be? If we got to history's end, what would we discover? That time and discourse had simply stopped? How then could we discover this? And why anyway would one want to get to such a point? Is the notion even intelligible?

Here let me make a detour, and talk about Hegel. The last great metaphysician of the Western tradition was, to be sure, a theological disaster. And yet theologians, including myself, keep returning to him. In my case, the attraction is Hegel's acute discernment of the *sort* of sense *history* makes, as against the sort a machine or an inductive system or a non-dissipative system makes. Hegel's famous logic of thesis, antithesis, and synthesis, *if* it is not deployed to constrain what is possible but is grasped rather as possibility's own pattern, is surely indeed the logic of specifically historical being. Thesis and antithesis are the conflicts that are definitive of created temporality, whether in the life of an individual, a civilization, or all creation. And the pattern comprised by each thesis and its antithesis, *"aufgehoben"* into a new historical configuration, taken up into and sublated by and into each new future, precisely fits history as the biblical record leads us to see it. Moreover, Hegel's construal works; it does let us see history's sense. The great instance of Hegel's time was of course the French revolution, when autocracy provoked popular sovereignty, which could be preserved only by an autocrat incorporating the will of the people.

Thus the one conceivable end of history, that will not cancel the whole being of history, must again be an *Aufhebung*. But into what? When creation ends, there is only one thing left to be taken into, and that of course is God. An end of history, if not a sheer nothing, could only be temporal history's *Aufhebung* into the infinite history that the Father and Son are between them in the Spirit. Whether or not proofs of God's existence work, that say the chains of causation have to start with something uncaused, it is, I think, plain that the chains of historical sublation will not make a whole history unless they eventuate in a sublation that is not itself sublated. Thus the doctrine of *theosis*, the doctrine that our end is inclusion in God's life, is not merely the brand of eschatology preferred by the Eastern churches; it names the only possible "end" of a *creation*, the only possible end of being that is history and drama.

This can be said, of course, only of a God who is himself a history, only of the God who is the archetype of thesis, antithesis, and synthesis, only of the triune God. We can only be taken into the life of a God who has a life to be taken into. One must indeed fear that many of those theologians who dislike the notion of deification misconstrue it because they do not at bottom conceive of God as alive in himself but rather as a timeless essence, so that being taken into God would mean exchanging one essence for another, would mean the abolition of humanity by divinity. But no more than being into a human family by adoption, is being taken into the life of Father, Son, and Spirit that kind of transformation.

I come to that explanation I promised earlier, of how one can tell a story about a single event. If the Great Transformation is not a series of events, but a single eternal event, how can you narrate it? Indeed, what would a single "eternal" event be?

The final event of our life with God will be our being taken fully into his own life. Now the point about God's life is that it is not stretched out on a time line *external* to him. There is no past to God's life, if by the past we mean what is back there at a different location on a time line than the present, so that we cannot get at it. And there is no future to God's life, if to have future is to be confronted as we are by advents that may break his unity with himself. But as God is the Father and the Spirit there *are* a Whence and a Whither in God; and as he is the Son there is a reconciliation of God's Whence and his Whither.

That is, there is a story of God's life, in that it has a plot. As to what plot actually is, whatever it might have been, it is the plot of the story the Bible tells. To be taken into God is to be taken into the living of our own creation and redemption, as in God nothing of the story ever is lost in the past or threatens from the future.

Readers will have noticed a certain desperation in these last attempts to bend language to a final description of God and a final description of our promised life in God. Also the great words of this century's trinitarian theology — "history," "event," "pure duration" — finally lose their purchase. At the end of the first volume of my systematic theology, I followed Jonathan Edwards in proposing that the final word about God is that he is beautiful, and that as he is the biblical God, who is Whence and Whither, he is beautiful with the kind of beauty that music has. Indeed, I proposed that he is beautiful with the kind of beauty that a certain *kind* of music has. The last word about God, I said, is that he is a great fugue, of Father, Son, and Spirit.

So the last word about us is this: the end is music. I have therefore asked a theologian in a different mode to finish my lecture for me. (When this paper was read as a lecture, an organist here played a Bach triple fugue.)

Prophetic and Apocalyptic Politics

PAUL D. HANSON

Introduction

This paper addresses only one aspect of the role of the Bible in the life of faith: its applicability to political process. To narrow our subject even further, we shall focus on two of the five political models that are found in the Bible, making only passing reference to the theocratic, the royal ("two swords"), and the sapiential models.

Underlying our reflections are two assumptions. I believe they are assumptions that are in harmony with an informed understanding of the Christian faith. The *first assumption* is that the Bible, taken as a whole and properly understood, reveals the nature of the relationship between God and creation that provides the foundation for all aspects of human existence, including the efforts of humans to construct just and equitable structures of governance. Proper understanding, however, includes recognition of the fact that biblical revelation does not take the form of specific political policies. If it did, it would be woefully outdated, since the political realities of the world today are vastly different from those of the time of the Davidic monarchy or the periods of Assyrian, Persian, and Roman hegemony. God's will is revealed in the Bible on a much more fundamental level as a call to mortals of every age to give up an anthropocentric worldview and to submit to a theocentric faith through repentance of human striving, acceptance of divine grace as sufficient for every need, and submission to the heavenly sovereign's universal purposes for all creation. Without this starting point of reconciliation with the divine purposer through ac-

43

ceptance of God's grace in faith, any talk of a biblically based political strategy will be doomed to take the form of just another human ideology. What is worse: If, as is so frequently the case, an ideological program becomes identified with divine will and becomes the foundation of a political strategy, it becomes idolatrous. This is the case no matter how noble its goals may be. The only position, then, that is true to Scripture is renunciation of allegiance to any human ideology that seeks to bind our conscience by presenting a political strategy as identical to divine will, regardless of whether it comes from the political left or right, whether it assumes a Marxist or a capitalist economic theory or any political ideology requiring ultimate commitment.

Biblical *politics* is a subject that one dare broach, therefore, only after having clarified the nature of biblical *theology*. According to the central tenets of biblical theology, political strategies that grow out of Scripture remain strictly epiphenomenal, that is, they are human responses to faith as faith seeks appropriate application in the concreteness of human existence. This is not to say that human politics are unimportant. The translation of faith into political action is consistent with the biblical principles of justice and mercy that lie at the heart of prophetic tradition and the teachings of Jesus. Or stated differently, the implications of biblical faith relate to every facet of life, since the universal sovereign's domain embraces all creation!

The narrative in 1 Samuel 12 gives expression to the crucial distinction between the application of faith to praxis mandated by biblical tradition and the idolatry that emerges when one structure of governance is identified with divine will. The chastened people of Israel came to Samuel, after they had been forced by events to acknowledge the validity of Samuel's earlier warnings that kingship would bring with it institutions that contradicted the ideals of their exodus faith, and they begged for forgiveness. His reply was incisive: Their ratification of kingship as their form of government was indeed a sinful decision. Yet he would not abandon them, but would continue to pray for the people *and* their king. Then he stated the crucial point: "Only fear the Lord, and serve him faithfully with all your heart; for consider what great things he has done for you. But if you still do wickedly, you shall be swept away, both you and your king" (1 Sam. 12:24-25).

In this passage we see the earliest clear formulation of the biblical principle regulating the relation between faith and politics. It revolves around the unambiguous distinction between the ultimate and the penultimate. The people should not have expected too much from kingship. As a human institution, it was tainted by sin, as is any form of government. Whether it would stand or fall depended on the way its affairs were ordered in relation to another regime, God's universal reign. Hence Samuel's admonition: "Only fear the Lord. . . ."

It is this distinction between ultimate and penultimate that forms the basis of St. Augustine's political theology. Martin Luther subsequently contributed the classical formulation of Samuel's "razor" in his so-called "two-kingdoms teaching."[1] For Luther it was obvious that until we commit ourselves in ultimate, unqualified allegiance to the exclusive reign of God over all reality, we are not free to render dependable service to our earthly government, whatever form it may assume.

The *second assumption* underlying this paper is as follows: God's revelation of God's self and of God's will occurred within the "thickness" of the life experiences of real humans in actual communities. This distinguishes biblical faith from the mythic religions of antiquity, which is to say, biblical faith relates to human regimes as matters of significance in God's plan for creation, whereas mythic cults denigrate human institutions to the status of mere reflections of heavenly realities. When we witness the leaders of ancient Israel shaping the life of the nation within the structures of theocracy, monarchy, or priestly hierocracy, or the early Christian community adapting life to Roman rule, we are observing ways in which faith or lack of faith gave rise to political strategies within concrete historical settings. It is within the biblical witness of such concrete political involvements that we can discern the emergence of religious and moral principles that contribute to our own efforts to formulate a suitable biblical political theology in our time.

These observations allow us to draw this conclusion: We will benefit greatly from studying the different political models found in the Bible if we are attentive to the cardinal biblical distinction between the ultimate and the penultimate and to the concreteness of the settings in which ancient Israel and the early Christian community trans-

---

1. Unfortunately, his "Zwei-Reichs Lehre" was distorted by the Nazi-dominated *Deutsche Kirche* into an ecclesiology that muted the prophetic role of the church in relation to the powers of state. Properly understood, the "two-kingdoms teaching" outlines a relationship between church and state that is both true to biblical principles and compatible with the First Amendment of the U.S. Constitution.

lated their ultimate faith-allegiance into penultimate political responsibilities. Such study does not produce a simple-minded platform of
biblical politics. What it does contribute is less direct but immeasur-
ably more important, namely, theological and moral principles that
provide the foundation for any Christian reflection on the role of faith
in political process and helpful guidelines regarding the modes of engagement suitable for different situations.

The Assault on Biblical Theology

Efforts to clarify the potential contribution of a critical understanding
of biblical tradition to contemporary political process have met a new
obstacle: Certain cultured despisers of theism have made a newly con-
certed assault on biblical faith by confusing Christianity with fundamentalism. And so they ask, "How can anyone be guided politically by
a body of literature that uses God as warrant for the indiscriminate
slaughtering of women and children, that supports the institution of
slavery, and that teaches a primitive form of the natural sciences?"
Unfortunately, fundamentalistically motivated creationist campaigns
like the one influencing the Kansas State Board of Education reinforce
the prejudices of those predisposed to identify religious faith with
myth or superstition. If such critics would take the time to study Martin Luther's distinction between *verba* and *scriptura*,[2] or, for that matter, bother to discuss biblical theology with any intelligent mainstream Christian, they would realize that classical Christianity has
been much more subtle in its application of Scripture to modern experience than the popular talk-show fundamentalists would lead them
to believe. It is simply wrongheaded to accuse biblical theologians in
the Lutheran, Roman Catholic, or Reformed traditions of a crude form
of biblical literalism and political positivism. But the spotlight of the
media is directed less frequently on responsible spokespersons of
Christian tradition than on the tirades of televangelists and the plati-
tudes of politicians. This can lead to the trivialization of religion in the
public forum, as noted by Stephen L. Carter,[3] which further encour-

2. Cf. Paul D. Hanson, "Biblical Authority Reconsidered," *Horizons in Biblical Theology* (1990): 57-79.

3. Stephen L. Carter, *The Culture of Disbelief: How American Law and Politics Trivialize
Religious Devotion* (New York: Basic Books, 1993).

ages the dismissal of biblical faith as a perspective to be taken seriously in political debate. Though the sources of the assault on traditional biblical religion are complex, one phenomenon will be singled out for closer scrutiny because of the breadth of its appeal, namely, postmodernism.

Though many differences in approach can be found among those who identify themselves as postmodernists or who apply the interpretive principles of deconstructionism, an overarching common trait is the repudiation of the efforts of modern individuals or communities to discern patterns of meaning in the (scriptural and other) monuments of the past that might shed light on contemporary experience. According to the cynicism of this line of thought, the modern individual or group must rely solely on its own creative insight and discourse. The result is a society cut off from the possibility of building upon common historical traditions and divided among separate collectivities, each laying claim to rights defended on the basis of its particularistic, self-interested, parochial conversation. In such a situation, elected and appointed representatives are stripped of the responsibility of identifying goals and instilling in the citizenship virtues capable of attaining the common good and must be confined to the tightly restricted function of refereeing conflicts as they inevitably and incessantly arise between groups sharing no sense of common values or goals.[4]

The damage being done by the epidemic of relativism arising from postmodernism is not limited to the field of religion. Chaos reigns in the humanities and social sciences in general. And how can it be otherwise once scholars and practitioners become convinced that the historical meaning of texts and other cultural artifacts no longer matters and the imagination of the modern interpreter trumps authorial intention as the source of understanding? One no longer looks for guidance to the classics of the past such as Scripture, since the doctrine of strict indeterminacy determines that each community of interpretation or even each individual interpreter is entitled to its own privileged interpretation. Truths are strictly private affairs. Communities can no longer be unified by a shared heritage, or even, in a pluralistic

4. An excellent analysis of the transformation from the republican political theory to that of a strictly "procedural democracy" is found in Michael J. Sandel, *Democracy's Discontent: America in Search of a Public Philosophy* (Cambridge, Mass.: Harvard University Press, 1996).

society, by the recognition of overlapping beliefs and values in the traditions of diverse communities — beliefs and values that can be embraced by broad consensus-building coalitions in the ongoing task of constructing a healthy society and maintaining the democratic institutions that safeguard liberty and equality.[5]

This hermeneutical solipsism has abetted the elevation of diversity from an undeniable fact of modern life to the status of an ideology, i.e., pluralism understood as a political dogma. Whether in the area of linguistics, culture, or morality, shared standards evaporate before the insistence that one individual's standard is as good as another's so long as it does not impinge on someone's rights.

To be sure, the patron saint of deconstructionism, Michel Foucault, was motivated by resistance to what he perceived — no doubt often justifiably — as the abuse of hegemonic power held by political and religious leaders. Deconstruct social and religious institutions so as to demonstrate that no unifying values can be retrieved from a past disaggregated into unconnected fragments and supposedly what will arise is a new free civilization. But how naïve this movement was to fail to recognize that the resulting chorus of interpreters, with each participant looking no further than its own self-invested imagination, would lead not to a free society but to the threat of anarchy. The reaction we are experiencing throughout the world is no accident. In the face of confusion, lost individuals are desperate to find certainties, and they quickly fall prey to fundamentalisms, rigid orthodoxies, and dictatorships. In liberal churches with little sense of history and consequently no compass to guide them into an uncertain future, defection rates are high, as members in search of meaning flock to sects that offer absolute truths (i.e., timeless fundamentals derived from a mythologized understanding of Scripture).

I find it ironic that right at the time many of my younger colleagues in the Harvard English department are rejecting deconstruction and returning to a vivid interest in author and setting, Walter Brueggemann publishes the first postmodernist theology of the Old Testament and Patrick D. Miller, the highly respected Old Testament scholar and brother-in-law of Professor Brueggemann, describes the work on the dust jacket as the "most important Old Testament theol-

5. Cf. Alasdair MacIntyre, *After Virtue: A Study in Moral Theory* (Notre Dame, Ind.: University of Notre Dame Press, 1981).

ogy to arise out of the American scene in this century."[6] Brueggemann presents the Bible as a courtroom in which witnesses present diverse portraits of God. God is an ever changing phenomenon, sometimes wrathful, sometimes forgiving, or to use one of Brueggemann's metaphors, "a loose cannon," a being with unpredictable mood changes. Unlike earlier biblical theologians, who accepted as part of their responsibility the explication of how the diverse portraits of God contribute ultimately to the confession of faith in the one true God (a responsibility taken seriously also by biblical authors like the Deuteronomist or Ezekiel), Brueggemann leaves it up to the reader to puzzle through the widely divergent views on the subject of deity in the Bible.

Brueggemann illustrates a tendency in recent theology to imitate popular cultural trends and adapt them to theological study right at the time when the culture shows signs of moving on to other interpretive models. A world suffering from the ravages of religious wars in the former Yugoslavia, in West Africa, Indonesia, and the Middle East, seeks from its religious communities neither the absolutism of the various fundamentalisms and ultra-orthodoxies nor the arbitrariness of religious relativism. How curious that the UN and NATO have made an about-face by applying their might to address questions concerning universal human rights precisely at the time when liberal communities of faith settle for religion robbed of its grounding in the universal God revealed in sacred traditions as the protector of the dignity of every human. People of faith are required to construct their lives against assumptions that in the world of natural science would destroy the basis of experimental research. Though faced with a far more complex universe than the neatly ordered machine of Newton, a microbiology lab could not conduct its business on the basis of the completely indeterminate world of postmodernism. I am further intrigued how the mysterious, infinitely complex, and yet unified world of I. I. Rabe, Albert Einstein, and Gerald Holton does not exclude, but invites sensitivity to transcendence as an important dimension of probing the mysteries of modern physics. It is high time for theologians to regain something of the sense of infinite mystery that is a

6. Walter Brueggemann, *Theology of the Old Testament: Testimony, Dispute, Advocacy* (Minneapolis: Fortress Press, 1997). For a review of Brueggemann's *Theology*, cf. Paul D. Hanson, "A New Challenge to Biblical Theology," *Journal of the American Academy of Religion* 67, no. 2 (1999): 447-59.

characteristic of human existence and that is central to the domain en-
trusted to them for interpretation within the wider society.

To conclude these comments on the assault of relativism introduced by postmodernism, I would venture to suggest that postmodernism has taken as its starting point a valid insight that has been
argued by philosophers in the hermeneutical tradition ever since
Schleiermacher and by historiographers since Collingwood: The old-
fashioned positivism of the Enlightenment is passé. For well-founded
philosophical and epistemological reasons, having to do especially
with the inescapable subjectivity of the inquirer, the interpreter of the
past can never reach certainty in his or her reconstruction. But where
the line from this valid starting point to the abyss of hermeneutical
and cultural chaos is transgressed is where the further argument is
made that one interpretation or reconstruction is as good as any other,
since unifying truth is denied *a priori* as a category. That line can be
passed not on the basis of scientific argument, but strictly on the basis
of presupposition. When we accept as our starting point a different
presupposition stemming from the classic confessions of the Christian faith, we need not feel philosophically any less credible. To the
contrary. Our voice may regain some of the authenticity of theologians
of a previous era, such as Paul Tillich and the Niebuhr brothers, as
theologians return to their rightful task of shedding light on life's
most profound mystery, its transcendental Source.

The Starting Point of a Christian Political Theology

A Christian political theology begins where all facets of Christian theology begin, with the central confessions of the faith.

"I believe in God the Father, Maker of Heaven and Earth." For the
Christian, reality is one, because its Creator is one. We face epistemological difficulties in understanding that one Reality, but this does not
compromise in the slightest the Christian confession that the oneness
of God is the foundation of everything we do on earth.

A central aspect of God's oneness is our encounter with God in
the concreteness of human history: "I believe in Jesus Christ, His only
Son, our Lord . . . who was crucified, was buried, and rose again. . . ."
Christians can contribute to healing within the political arenas of this
world because of God's initiative in Christ to call into being a forgiven

and reconciled community of faith. To obscure the etiology of the church in divine grace by placing at center stage human skills (be they political, medical, administrative, or whatever) is to destroy the unique contribution that faith-based communities have to make to political process and to confuse their role with that of publicly funded agencies and volunteer organizations.

"And I believe in the Holy Spirit. . . ." Even in the epiphenomenal, penultimate, alien world that lies on the unfinished side of God's universal kingdom, we are not alone, but sustained by God's presence. God's Spirit is present in every faithful community — however large or small — that labors on behalf of God's mercy and justice. People of faith who labor in the political sphere, whether as full-time professionals or as ordinary citizens, recognize the Spirit as more active and powerful and real than any human force. From this recognition they derive freedom and courage to stand for justice, even when that position is unpopular or dangerous.

Prophetic Politics

Five political models are represented in the Old Testament. Two of them, theocracy and monarchy, we shall merely allude to. One we shall skip over entirely (the sapiential model). The remaining two constitute the twin themes of our remaining discussion.

Early Israel began as a theocracy. Arguably, theocracy is the polity most ideally suited for a people seeking to pattern its political life after divine purpose. It dissolves the distinction between God's rule and human rule. The two are identified under the leadership of one designated by God's spirit to lead for the length of time that the charismatic designation remains manifest. Theocracy is in effect the polity designed to embody the kingdom of God in the communal life of the faithful on earth. In a real sense, it is the state for which the pious of all ages have prayed.

As in the case in attempts to enact theocracy throughout the ages and down to modern times (e.g., states like Iran and Pakistan), the people of ancient Israel encountered difficulties in translating the ideals of theocracy into the pragmatics of historical existence. One difficulty was the tenure of leaders who degraded the effects of the divine charisma by succumbing to the lure of self-aggrandizing power and personal greed. Another difficulty was the inability of a dispirited theocracy to defend itself against military powers like the Philistines. Theocracy accordingly collapsed and was replaced by monarchy, though the inner yearning for God's rule mediated by an inspirited godly leader never died.

Kingship, the second political model to be adopted by Israel, was the preeminent polity of antiquity. Its durability came not by the identification of human rule with divine through temporary, charismatic leaders, but by its linking a permanent structure of human governance (a royal dynasty) to divine patronage. Subjects think twice before opposing a leader touted as a divine deputy!

It was the adoption of kingship that, from the perspective of *Realpolitik*, saved Israel from annihilation. Nevertheless, of all five political models, monarchy created the most difficulties for biblical faith. The reason was its obscuring the boundary between divine and human authority. To understand why any encroachment on divine authority was held deeply suspect in Israel, one need only recall Israel's origins in slavery under a self-declared divine Pharaoh. The Hebrews were delivered from eternal slavery by the categorical repudiation of all claims for divinity made by human potentates. This repudiation and its positive formulation, the command to acknowledge one God alone, were etched into Hebrew consciousness for all time. Divine kingship contradicted the historical ontology of which Jewish identity was constructed.

The third political model in the Bible is the most significant one. It is the prophetic model. However, it is not an autonomous model, but a parasite. It lives in relation to an earthly regime, as seen by the fact that prophecy arose with kingship in Israel and ceased with monarchy's demise. Yet prophecy embodies nothing less than the essence of Israel's religious contribution to political theory, namely, the claim that human politics, in contrast to divine politics, can never be exact, but only proximate, never ultimate, but only penultimate, never self-generating, but only derivative, never eternal, but only transient. But this is to construe it in negative terms. Stated positively, the prophetic political model embodies the primacy of faith over human agency and temporal institutions. It thus comports with what we identified above as the starting point of any biblically based reflection of political theology, the oneness of reality grounded in the oneness of God. As we shall illustrate from the prophetic corpus, the prophets entered every political dialogue by stating clearly the necessary grounding of every political strategy in submission to God's universal suzerainty. Complete trust in God was the quality without which prophetic politics was impossible. The inevitable concomitant of the ascription of absolute rule to God alone was the relativization of every human institution.

It is the peripatetic, parasitic quality of prophetic politics that made it the most adaptable and long-lived of the biblical models. It is the model that biblical tradition handed down to subsequent ages that proved to be applicable to diverse types of human governance in a manner roughly analogous to the software one installs in one's computer to protect operating programs against destructive viruses. But enough of clever analogies. What are the cardinal characteristics of the prophetic model?

The prophetic model is the contribution *par excellence* of ethical monotheism to political theory. To understand this, one must understand the prevailing view in antiquity: that an enduring political system's authority was based on identity with divine rule, a feature we noted earlier to be especially prominent in monarchy. This involved two facets. First, the political leader was presented as the designated deputy of the deity, a concept often construed in terms of divine sonship and implying a prerogative handed down from father to son (hence, dynastic succession). Second, the imperial cult manifested the special status of the nation by virtue of the presence of the patron deity's image in the central sanctuary. Two important political consequences arose from these strategies: The political leadership was permanent and beyond human reproof, and the nation enjoyed special entitlements within the family of nations relating to trade and conquest.

Prophetic politics, while refusing to endorse any political ideology as identical with God's eternal rule, does have a very clear identifying mark in relation to divine rule, namely, it demands of all people of faith — regardless of their host governments — unqualified allegiance to God's universal domain. It manifests its loyalty to that domain by preserving and handing down the story of the divine sovereign's acts on behalf of all humans and by promulgating the mercy code *(torah)* that the community of faith inferred from that story and embellished over time.

It is on the basis of that story and that mercy code that those entering political activity guided by the prophetic model have engaged their respective societies and regimes. No political leader and no nation has been exempt from their moral scrutiny and critique. This negative judgment rests upon the more important positive confession: There is only one universal, true governance, and that is the reign of the one true God. From that reign and the imperatives it implies are derived the moral standards against which every ruler and every nation are judged.

True prophets of every age have thus addressed their compatriots as spokespersons of this universal divine reign. As Amos's call indicates, such spokespersons represented no special class, but rather arose from the populace: "I am no prophet, nor a prophet's son; but I am a herdsman, and a dresser of sycamore trees, and the Lord took me from following the flock, and the Lord said to me, 'Go, prophesy to my people Israel'" (Amos 7:14-15). The distinguishing mark of the prophet was that he or she spoke not out of personal or partisan interest but solely on behalf of the universal suzerain by whom the prophet was called to service: "The lion has roared; who will not fear? The Lord God has spoken; who can but prophesy?" (Amos 3:8).

Prophetic politics then is the activity of those who have received the divine call to advocate for the standards of universal divine reign that transcends all human boundaries. It is impossible to understand prophecy until one grasps their sense of that divine reign. Here the temptation is to be guided by the popular connotation of prophet as untraditional individualist. Wrong on both accounts! The prophet is one who preserves the central tenets of his or her faith tradition and gives expression to them out of a sense of solidarity with his or her community. But advocacy and critique based on the community's tradition does not rest on the reification of tradition; it rests on the belief that contained within that tradition is a faithful (albeit imperfect and incomplete) witness to the will of the universal sovereign.

Again Amos serves as an example. First, he calls Israel to account for its egregious moral wrongs by holding its behavior up against the torah tradition extrapolated from its epic account of God's saving activity (Amos 2:6-16). Second, he undercuts the false sense of security that Israel enjoys by attacking its nationalist cult as a strictly human product that will be obliged to submit to the egalitarian standards of universal divine justice (Amos 5:18-24).

The starting point of prophetic politics in the central confessions of Yahwistic faith is illustrated also by the prophet Isaiah. In chapter one he pronounces divine judgment upon a nation that derives its sense of security from the rituals of its national cult. God holds only disdain for a national(istic) cult that uses the motions of ritual to shield itself from the straightforward demands of social justice associated with God's reign. Violence and ritual piety are categorically incompatible.

Isaiah was consistent as well in applying the central faith principle to international politics. King Ahaz was determined to base his policy in relation to the Assyrian Empire on the familiar, pragmatic political strategy of balance of power. Over against this Isaiah presented a divine mandate: "Unless you act on the basis of faith, you will not be established" (Isa. 7:9). Later in the century, when King Hezekiah was tempted to turn to Egypt as the best remedy against the Assyrian Emperor Sennacherib's threat, Isaiah commended the same starting point in faith: "For thus said the Lord God, the Holy One of Israel. 'In returning and rest you shall be saved; in quietness and in trust shall be your strength'" (Isa. 30:15).

Granted, the prophet's insistence that a dependable domestic or foreign policy must begin with a clear acknowledgment of the primacy of faith will not produce a timeless blueprint for such policy. But the prophet's task is not that of the civil servant or statesman trained to craft the details of welfare policy or draft the terms of international treaties. The prophet's task is to remind a nation that its structures of governance are not identical with divine rule and that if it is to survive it must articulate both domestic and foreign policy in terms consistent with moral principles that transcend partisan politics and nationalistic self-interest by being derived from God's universal imperium. Therefore Isaiah informed Ahaz in no uncertain terms of the existence of a power that he should fear infinitely more than the power of either Syria and Assyria (8:13). What stood in the way of such properly placed fear? Pride, the prophet replied, which more than any other human attitude exposes individual and nation to calamity (2:12-17; cf. 14:12-20). In the place of pride, the prophet urged quiet trust in God and keen awareness that the universal reign that transcends every earthly government was the only adequate starting point for doing politics.

Inevitably the prophets were, in the fashion of Socrates, political gadflies. They had few friends in high places, because they were intimidated by no blustery potentate and surrendered conscience to no earthly ruler. They could not be purchased. On behalf of the universal sovereign they spoke with a consistency and courage that rattled earthly kings and their obsequious high priests (Amos 7:10-17). Like Amos, Jeremiah could stand up to the king and declare that the king was betraying his sacred trust by placing his own comfort over the administration of evenhanded justice to his subjects (Jer. 22:11-19). He could be equally scathing in his attack on a national cult that took comfort in the assurances of unconditional divine protection unaffected by the state's gross neglect of its responsibilities to uphold the rights of its citizens (Jer. 7).

Though our focus here is on the Old Testament, it is fitting to observe that throughout his life Jesus of Nazareth embodied commitment to God's universal sovereignty. His willingness to die to preserve the primacy of the claims of God's kingdom on every facet of human activity not only kept alive the witness of Israel's prophets but, through the resurrection, announced for all time a righteous dominion to which every human regime would ultimately be obliged to submit. What was anticipated already in Old Testament prophecy and apocalyptic (e.g., Isa. 52:13–53:12; Dan. 12:1-4) became explicit in the disciples' experience of their risen Lord: Because of the resurrection, the one committed to God's universal reign could dedicate his or her energies courageously and selflessly to nation and world with the quiet confidence that justice and mercy were the only policies that finally would prevail.

To summarize the points we have made about prophetic politics: Prophetic politics is not a political platform, but a political posture assumed by members of a given society who give expression to their patriotism by ascribing to their government limited, penultimate authority, while reserving their ultimate allegiance for the universal sovereign, the Creator God of all nations. Their contribution to the health and prosperity of nation, world, and universe is not diminished but enhanced by the conditions their faith places on their patriotism, for through it they help a society maintain the kind of moral foundation without which any nation is doomed to moral bankruptcy and implosion. The Christian who understands and applies the biblical prophetic dialectic to his or her particular setting represents the kind of citizenship that is critically important but woefully rare in most societies, a citizenship embodying the courage and moral rigor that refuses to be co-opted by any partisan or ideological position.

In day-to-day life, prophetic politics is given direction by its most classic formulation: "Thy kingdom come, thy will be done, on earth as it is in Heaven." In the Lord's Prayer we hear eloquently and suc-cinctly the critical distinction between the ultimate and the penulti-mate that distinguishes prophetic politics from other political move-ments. The same clarity comes to expression in another familiar Jesus word, which we might apply to our specific topic by this adaptation: "Strive first for the kingdom of God and his righteousness and reliable political policy will follow" (cf. Matt. 6:33).

In the history of biblical communities, men and women of faith maintained the standards of God's domain as the measure against which all political policies, foreign or domestic, were measured. In pe-riods in which leaders of government and society were open to their critique, prophecy flourished, as during the reigns of Jehoshaphat, He-zekiah, and Josiah. More frequently, the prophets were ignored or de-nounced, but so long as they were able, they continued to proclaim God's righteousness and mercy on behalf of all who suffered under re-pression and greed. At such times, however, when their every word or act on behalf of God's domain was met by violent persecution and death, men and women of faith adopted another political strategy, namely, apocalyptic politics.

Apocalyptic Politics

The model of apocalyptic politics arose in those periods of biblical his-tory where the faithful had no opportunity to give public testimony to the religious principles and moral values they believed to be mandated by their ultimate allegiance to the universal reign of God. In more nor-mal periods in which the model of prophetic politics could be applied by members of the faith community, instances of injustice and unfaith-fulness had a finite quality and were addressed by admonitions and warnings aimed at reform. But what happens in times when any effort at reform based on the standards of justice and compassion associated with God's reign are repulsed by violence and persecution? Examples of such times were the reign of terror under Antiochus IV Epiphanes (2nd c. B.C.E.), the persecution of Jews and Christians under Nero and Domitian, and in modern times the extermination of Jews and their Christian supporters under the Nazis. Out of the Nazi Holocaust arose the witness of Dietrich Bonhoeffer, who saw in the unspeakable horrors of genocide an assault on the kingdom of God that could be described in the apocalyptic terms of the attack of the Antichrist.

Mention of the Antichrist may have a mythological ring in our modern ears. But that is simply because we are so accustomed to security and comfort as not to be able to comprehend apocalyptic horrors. But sadly history has frequently witnessed situations in which Evil has manifested itself in a shape larger than individual humans or temporal regimes. Even indirect encounter with such situations can be traumatizing. An illustration may be helpful.

In the fall of 1982 our family was on a sabbatical leave in Munich, Germany. Against the sound counsel of my wife, I insisted that children born to Lutheran parents were obliged to be exposed to the horrors of a concentration camp. So off the family of five went to Dachau. After the sites of camps and gas chambers and — far worse — the picture galleries of gaunt faces and wasted bodies had been visited, our son Mark, age eight, was deeply distressed. For weeks, he was awakened in the middle of the night by apparitions of Adolf Hitler chasing him into a gas chamber. Mark had witnessed Evil-exceeding-human-form at Dachau, that is, he had witnessed the Antichrist. In the terms of our present study, he was in need of a symbolization of reality that differed from the activism of prophetic politics, with its delegation of responsibility for translating the qualities of God's reign into human experience to human agents. He was in need of a vision of God's *direct* intervention to defeat Antichrist in places that seemed overcome by the forces of Evil. Fortunately, he received such a vision through the uncommon grace of a Holocaust survivor who providentially introduced himself to us as we waited for the Munich train and in a narrative comprehensible to children described a power greater than the most horrible human cruelty, the power of love.

Apocalyptic politics came to the aid of communities in the biblical period under the dire circumstances in which their prophets were forced out of the public square into the sanctuary of clandestine conventicles. *In extremis,* such communities, whether in biblical or modern times, like the mortally wounded soldier suffering excruciating pain, need a more potent antidote than the normal remedy. Their need can be addressed only by apocalyptic visions assuring them that all appearances notwithstanding, God remains sovereign and God's righteous reign will prevail.

The apocalyptic seer's calling thus is different from that of the prophet. While sharing the same point of origin in an inaugural vision of God's universal reign, it does not lead to the prophetic commissioning to a career of involvement in political process, but encourages the cultivation of communities of support that allow their members to persevere in faith under the protection of anonymity. Apocalyptic seers linger longer in their visions of Heaven than prophets and describe in greater detail the transcendent drama that gives the suffering human communities assurance that the victory being secured in Heaven against the principalities and powers of Evil will one day be conferred upon them as well. Apocalyptic politics is a gift from God to the persecuted communities of every age that experience the execution of their leaders and the slaughter of their children, be it in Rome in the last half of the first century or Germany in the early 1940s.

In the history of biblical Israel, the apocalyptic political model was applied in two different situations: (1) by members of an oppressed religious minority suffering at the hands of their nation's own religious and political elite; (2) by citizens of the Jewish nation suffering persecution inflicted by an occupying foreign power. Of course, the distinction is often blurred, as in the Maccabean period when Jewish collaborators frequently joined cause with the foreign oppressor.

An example of the apocalyptic model applied to a situation of internecine strife is found in Isaiah 56–66.[7] The suffering minority summarizes the bleak situation of their community thus:

> Justice is turned back, and righteousness stands at a distance;
> For truth stumbles in the public square, and uprightness cannot
>   enter.
> Truth is lacking, and whoever turns from evil is despoiled.
>
> (59:14-15a)

Of course, dishonest judges and corrupt political leaders were evils against which the prophets also railed. But while never hesitating to remind their listeners that their threats were backed up by the divine Judge, the prophets nevertheless persisted in the political process of addressing the nation's leaders and urging the powerful of the land to return to the just administration of their assigned duties. In contrast, apocalyptic seers, witnessing the plight of victims of persecution

7. This subject is covered in detail in Paul D. Hanson, *The Dawn of Apocalyptic*, 2nd ed. (Philadelphia: Fortress Press, 1979).

stripped of any political leverage and facing sure death as the consequence of protest, proclaim as a source of hope for their beleaguered
followers the vision of God's intervention to vindicate the oppressed
and to destroy the wicked:

> The Lord saw it, and it displeased him that there was no justice.
> He saw that there was no one, and was appalled that there was
>   no one to intervene;
> So his own arm brought him victory, and his righteousness upheld
>   him. (59:15b-16)

The apocalyptic model comes to the aid of an oppressed minority
by addressing the conceptual dissonance between its spiritual identity
as God's elect and its historical experience of suffering at the hands of
what it deems to be ungodly leadership. Of course, one alternative
would be to admit that it had erred and accommodate its beliefs to
historical circumstances. More often, however, its sectarian outlook is
preserved with the help of an apocalyptic worldview. The experienced
adversity is temporary and is to be understood as a time of trial to test
their perseverance. To their spiritual leaders God reveals visions of direct intervention through which they would be restored to positions
of honor and dignity, even as the opposition would be removed
through the execution of divine judgment (66:15-16).

It is not hard to understand how the apocalyptic political model
can lead to disengagement from the social and political structures of
society. Human government is fallen beyond rescue. It will be sup-
planted by divine governance. Patient endurance rather than reforming activity was the mode of obedience called for.

As we turn next to the second kind of situation to which the
model of apocalyptic politics was applied, Daniel 7–12 serves as a biblical example of apocalyptic politics operating in response to persecution perpetrated by an occupying foreign power. Historical events
have subjected the faithful to horrors of such a magnitude as to call
into question the validity of their belief that God was committed to
protecting those who remain faithful to the covenant. They witnessed
the execution of the most courageous among the Jews who refused to
submit to the demands of Antiochus IV Epiphanes, the zealous
Hellenizer from Antioch, that they renounce their Mosaic identity and
blend into the Greek culture.

The visions of Daniel 7–12 focus on a plane transcending the world of persecution and the victory of Evil. As described in chapter 7, a pitched battle in heaven has entered its final stages in which the patron powers of the earth's ruthless empires are being destroyed. The faithful thereby have assurance that it is only a matter of time before the heavenly victory of the Ancient One will be manifest on earth and eternal dominion will be given to the Son of Man. The faithful accordingly can assume an attitude of indifference towards the political structures of their immediate environment. Efforts to change them would be senseless, since the notion of changing temporal structures that are destined for destruction by God is absurd from an apocalyptic point of view. This does not rule out the fittingness of martyrdom, but that act of ultimate sacrifice, rather than being viewed as instrumental in changing present structures, must be construed as witnessing to the fact that this world of the flesh is but an illusion and that the world to come alone is real (12:1-4).

Though there is no evidence within the Scriptures that are canonical in the West for a transformation of apocalyptic politics into an activist mode, traces of this development are to be seen in the sectarian writings of the apocalyptic community at Qumran and in the apocalyptic rhetoric that was a part of the Jewish revolts against the Romans in AD 66-70 and AD 132-135. The *War Rule* from Qumran is particularly interesting, and puzzling, for it provides instructions for the preparation and conduct of the final eschatological battle in which those faithful to the covenant would join the hosts of heavenly angels. Were these instructions intended as spiritual exercises only, in which case they could still be interpreted as consistent with the pacifism of the canonical apocalyptic writings? Or were the weapons described and the strategies of war outlined intended for the conduct of actual war against the *kittim* (i.e., Romans). Whatever the original intent, it is clear that within a few decades the apocalyptic political model was being adapted to strategies of resistance and revolt that played an active role in the world in which Jesus of Nazareth was active and that subsequently would have profound effects on the development of Western civilization.

Concluding Theological Reflections on
Prophetic and Apocalyptic Politics

A description of prophetic and apocalyptic politics such as we have given may seem quite removed from the pressing issues currently confronting the church. But we should not be deceived by naïve arguments regarding relevancy. Sometimes it is wise to step back long enough from the immediate to fill in the background necessary to understand the true nature of "in-the-face" realities. And for a community built upon a scriptural foundation, it seems particularly important to take the time necessary both to clarify the biblical principles bearing on moral issues and to seek to understand what bearing the Bible has on the question of the strategies used in addressing political process. Since the emphasis in this paper has been on the latter, our summary reflections focus on the implications of our study for the activities of the church in relation to politics.

With the mention of apocalyptic in our modern setting, thoughts turn immediately to the sensationalizing hoopla generated by the media in the closing months of 1999 in connection with the premature celebration of the new millennium. But there is a far more important political dimension to apocalyptic that has the potential of setting the stage for violent conflict in the twenty-first century. For various reasons too complicated to be treated here, but certainly including the longing for religious certainties in an age of resurgent secularism and moral relativism, apocalyptic political strategies of the militant activist variety are being adopted by zealous leaders in most of the world religions. The common goal directing such efforts is the preservation of traditional cultures from inner decay and foreign conquest. For example, Sheik Hassan Nasrallah, Shiite Muslim cleric of the Party of God (*Hezbollah*), calls the faithful to Holy War against Israel in the name of Allah. The response of ultra-orthodox Judaism to Shiite fundamentalism is equally apocalyptic and violent, as seen in groups like the *Gush enunim* and the Kahanists. Most Christian versions of apocalyptic politics have not been as overtly explicit in plotting violence, though the apocalyptic element is present in certain paramilitary groups. While the apocalypticism of Jim Jones or David Koresh can perhaps be explained in part in pathological terms (though one must not use that explanation as an excuse shielding the normative society from the indictments implicit in their personal and communal tragedies), the enormously popular works of Hal Lindsey require another kind of analysis.[8] Basically, what is involved there is a categorical confusion between the two political models we have described.

On the basis of the study of the apocalyptic model in Scripture, one can confidently state that it was a model reserved for those who found themselves in situations of such extreme persecution that the prophetic model of translating the justice and mercy associated with God's reign into the institutions and structures of society was categorically unviable. The turn to the apocalyptic mode of awaiting God's intervention to judge the oppressor was strictly a recourse *in extremis.* When commended to citizens living in a land where through vote, protest, and civic involvement ample opportunities exist to translate faith into political action, adoption of the apocalyptic mode is nothing less than abdication of moral responsibility and escapism into a refuge that should be reserved for the victims of inescapable persecution. Though Hal Lindsey's followers, so far as I know, do not form apocalyptic armies in the manner of the Party of God or the *Gush enunim,* the cultivation of a death wish for humanity through lurid portrayal of the destruction of all flesh in God's imminent battle as the backdrop for the final bliss awaiting those who follow the instructions of the modern War Rule, *Late Great Planet Earth,* is itself in my mind an act of violence, violence against the human soul.

The two monumental apocalyptic writings in the Bible, Daniel and the Book of Revelation, indicate in unmistakable terms the conditions under which the application of apocalyptic politics is fitting. Tragically, modern history provides ample commentary on this biblical lesson, as it chronicles Dietrich Bonhoeffer describing his times in terms of the attack of the Antichrist and Hans Lilje writing his commentary on the Book of Revelation in the midst of his struggles against the Nazis and their collaborating bishops and clergy. In all cases, whether in biblical or in modern times, the starting point for those adopting the mode of apocalyptic politics was the same as the starting point of the prophets, namely, unqualified commitment to God's reign. Daniel, John of Patmos, Bonhoeffer, and Lilje acted as representatives of God's reign as they proclaimed to those being persecuted for the faith that all earthly appearances notwithstanding, the

---

8. Cf. Paul D. Hanson, *Old Testament Apocalyptic* (Nashville: Abingdon Press, 1987), pp. 55-58.

victory of God's kingdom over all evil was assured. The vividness of their visionary depictions of that victory thus was commensurate with the extreme crises that they addressed. When viewed against the classic Jewish and Christian expressions of apocalyptic politics, it is not difficult to recognize apocalyptic writings and movements that stem not from commitment to God's universal reign of justice and compassion but from the lust for human power and the perversion of religion into an instrument of crude self-centered fantasizing.[9]

It is noteworthy that no popular treatment of prophecy has come close to the marketing success of Lindsey's apocalyptic ravings. The reason is not that high-quality works expositing the prophetic option in language comprehensible to the general public do not exist, but rather, I suspect, it has to do with the fact that the prophetic message of the Bible places on communities and individuals demands of time, money, and energy. By contrast, popular works on apocalyptic produced by charlatans can be enjoyed, roughly in the manner of science fiction, from one's easy chair and within the safe confines of one's imagination. However, since the church's goal is not to win popularity contests but to be an obedient servant of God's reign, it need not be swayed by publishers' marketing reports.

What can be stated with a certainty is this: Given the circumstances within which the church exists in most parts of the Western world today, the biblical model that should guide its interaction with society and world is the prophetic model. To insure that that interaction is faithful to its mandate, it must begin with clarity concerning the primacy of its membership in the reign of God and the consequent derivative nature of all that it does in the world. To make this claim is not to imply that there are not faith communities in other parts of the world that live under adverse circumstances for which the apocalyptic model is fitting and proper. As we have noted, biblical faith has been guided by the search for the fitting expression of its beliefs and values within the concreteness of particular settings. We are therefore only suggesting that our historical and geographical location calls for a prophetic response of faithful commitment and moral engagement. How long that will be the case we can never know.

Once the church is clear about the prophetic mandate to which it

9. In *The Late Great Planet Earth*, Hal Lindsey's pop term for the rapture is "the ultimate trip."

is called, it finds itself equipped with a *modus operandi* that minimizes inertia and releases the potential it has for contributing to society. In the first instance, it brings into clear focus the centrality of worship as the place where its sacramental identity is secured. In the second instance, it finds through the word and its exposition the moral principles that form the basis for appropriate action. What action follows cannot be specified in generalities. At times the church may be led to corporate action. In others, it will recognize that the appropriate agents of prophetic action are individual members in their various vocations and stations in society. This is so because the prophetic political model does not furnish programs and policies applicable to all situations, but rather a style of responsiveness rooted in God's reign and directed at a world created by God and saved from self-destruction by God's redemptive act in Christ.

It is reported that James Muilenberg, beloved Old Testament professor of an earlier generation at Union Theological Seminary in New York, recommended to his students that they do biblical theology by holding Scripture in one hand and the *New York Times* in the other. As I complete this article, I have a clipping next to my keyboard that I found in this morning's *New York Times* (February 17, 2000). The first thirteen pages of the A-Section gave ample examples of the concrete settings within which the church, as God's servant people, is called upon to bear testimony on behalf of the justice and compassion of God's reign: Refugees staring at the ruins of their Grozny homes, indictments for money laundering in a New York bank, stalled peace processes in both Northern Ireland and Israel, ongoing strife in Sri Lanka. How heartening then to turn to page fourteen and discover a lesson in prophetic politics. There Gustav Niebuhr describes a statement issued by an ecumenical gathering in our nation's capital organized by Jim Wallis. The statement, entitled "Covenant to Overcome Poverty," is based on the biblical theme of obligation to the poor. It observes, "When you have rising inequality and record prosperity at the same time, it's a biblical issue." It recognizes that neither the church alone, nor government alone, will solve the problem. It does not detail specific policies. It does ask people to evaluate the policies advanced by political candidates on the basis of their biblically based faith commitments. Niebuhr's article, with its straightforward title "Christians Ask Renewed Attack on Poverty" may not register as highly on a scintillation register as Lindsey's *Late Great Planet Earth*.

But whereas Lindsey exposes Christianity to the scorn and dismissal of cultured despisers of religion, Niebuhr describes clearly how a proper grasp of biblical faith can provide the basis for the responsible participation in the democratic process of one of the religious communities in a highly diverse modern state. That community is the church of Jesus Christ, and its guiding model for political engagement at this point in time is the prophetic model.

Eschatology in the New Testament: The Current Debate

ARLAND J. HULTGREN

Prior to engaging our topic and issues related to it, some definitions and broad perspectives are in order. Once these are settled, two major positions on a particular aspect of eschatology in the New Testament will be taken up. And then some observations and critique will follow.

I. Definitions and Perspectives

We begin with some definitions. Eschatology has to do with beliefs about "the last things." But within current literature on eschatology in the New Testament one finds a host of adjectival modifiers attached to the term: cosmic eschatology, individual eschatology, prophetic eschatology, consistent or thoroughgoing eschatology, apocalyptic eschatology, realized eschatology, present eschatology, future eschatology, and now even "sapiential eschatology," and more. So where does one begin?

By way of generalization, it can be said that within biblical and non-canonical literature from antiquity, both Jewish and Christian, a distinction is often made between the present age, the period of history in which life is being lived, and a future, coming age, a period of transformed existence that God will bring about — either within history or beyond it. That new age is sometimes called the age to come, the messianic age, or the kingdom of God. The term "eschatology" is applied to that mode of thinking of two eras or ages. The term is a comprehensive one, and it must be, since there are different kinds of eschatology in the sources available to us. The term can refer to teaching about events expected to take place within a new era of history that will dawn, such as the return of exiles to their homeland; it can refer to teaching about events expected during the last days of history, such as wars and rumors of wars, earthquakes, famines, and apostasy; it can refer to things anticipated in the age to come, such as scenes around the heavenly throne and the descent of the New Jerusalem; or it can refer to all of these.[1]

The terms "eschatology" and "eschatological" are modern. In spite of the fact that one can speak of eschatology in the New Testament and in the teachings of major figures, such as Joachim of Flora, Martin Luther, and Thomas Müntzer, neither the New Testament nor any major figures prior to the modern era would have recognized the word "eschatology." The word was apparently coined in the seventeenth century, when the Lutheran dogmatician Abraham Calovius (1612-86) of Wittenberg used the term "Eschatologia Sacra" as a general heading at the end of his twelve-volume dogmatics published in 1677. Under that heading he dealt with the topics of death, resurrection, judgment, and consummation. But the term did not catch on and gain widespread use in German theology until well into the nineteenth century.[2] Even Friedrich Schleiermacher (1768-1834), in his work on *The Christian Faith* published in the early 1820s, remarked on it as a strange term.[3] The word does not appear in English usage until the middle of the nineteenth century.[4] But once the term came into the theological vocabulary, there was a new conceptual tool, and it became possible to think differently about the biblical message and figures within the New Testament, such as John the Baptist and Jesus. To think of them as eschatological prophets was a fresh conceptuality — a paradigm shift, as we like to say — allowing for something quite new.

1. The definition here is essentially that of Nancy L. Lapp, "Eschatology," *The HarperCollins Bible Dictionary*, rev. ed., ed. Paul J. Achtemeier (San Francisco: Harper-Collins, 1996), p. 302.

2. Erwin Fahlbusch, "Eschatologie," *Evangelisches Kirchenlexikon*, ed. E. Fahlbusch et al., 5 vols. (Göttingen: Vandenhoeck & Ruprecht, 1986-97), vol. 1, p. 1107.

3. Friedrich Schleiermacher, *The Christian Faith*, 2 vols. (New York: Harper & Row, 1963), vol. 2, p. 703 (first German ed., 1821-22).

4. *The Oxford English Dictionary*, 2nd ed., ed. J. A. Simpson and E. S. C. Weiner, 20 vols. (Oxford: Clarendon Press, 1989), vol. 5, p. 388. The earliest entry is from 1844.

The term "apocalyptic" refers to a particular kind of eschatology. A basic definition of apocalyptic has been offered by Paul Hanson. According to him, it consists of a "dualistic view of divine deliverance, entailing destruction of this world and resurrection of the faithful to a blessed heavenly existence."[5] Apocalyptic is therefore a more narrow term, referring to a particular kind of eschatology that expects an era beyond the present age of historical occurrences. Apocalyptic requires that both nature and history — the present world as we know it — make room for a new world that is perfected and eternal.

Within the current scene there is little debate around the question whether the New Testament is eschatological. It is conventional to say that the New Testament writings set forth various and differing eschatologies, to be sure, but that they are all eschatological in one way or another. Whether one is referring to the Synoptic Gospels, the letters of Paul, the Gospel of John, or any other portion, it is agreed that the New Testament is eschatological in one sense or another.

A quick inventory may be in order. The Gospel of Mark sets forth an imminent eschatological perspective. The parousia of the Son of Man is expected (8:38; 13:26), and the kingdom of God is to come "with power" during the first generation of the followers of Jesus (Mark 9:1).[6] The Gospel of Matthew shares the view of an imminent expectation. Moreover, it portrays the final judgment scene when all the nations will be gathered before the Son of Man, who will separate those before him as a shepherd separates the sheep from the goats (Matt. 25:31-46). Those on the one side will inherit the kingdom prepared for them, while those on the other side will be sent into eternal punishment. The Gospel of Luke entertains the possibility of a delay of the parousia before the coming of the Son of Man and other end-time events (cf. 19:11; 9:27 [against Mark 9:1]; 12:45; 17:20-21), but his coming and his exercising of authority in a final judgment are certain.[7]

The letters of the apostle Paul are also eschatological in outlook.

5. Paul D. Hanson, "Apocalypses and Apocalyptic," *The Anchor Bible Dictionary*, ed. David N. Freedman, 6 vols. (New York: Doubleday, 1992), vol. 1, p. 281.

6. On the imminent expectation of the parousia in Mark, cf. Willi Marxsen, *Mark the Evangelist: Studies on the Redaction History of the Gospel* (Nashville: Abingdon Press, 1969), pp. 195, 205. On Mark 8:38; 9:1; and 13:26, cf. Eduard Schweizer, *The Good News According to Mark* (Richmond: John Knox Press, 1970), pp. 177-79, 275.

7. Luke's eschatology was explored in the pioneering work of Hans Conzelmann, *The Theology of St. Luke* (New York: Harper & Brothers, 1960), see p. 150 in particular.

Paul declares that not all of his readers will die before the coming of the Lord. In both 1 Thessalonians 4 and 1 Corinthians 15 the apostle portrays the end of all things, including the coming of the Lord, the resurrection of the dead, and ultimately the triumph of God, who will be all in all. Moreover, with Paul there is not only the future eschatological view, the "not yet," but also the "already" of the new age inaugurated on Easter. Whoever is in Christ is a new creation already (2 Cor. 5:17).

The Fourth Gospel has its own kind of eschatology, even though it has clear relationships with the other two. On the one hand, it preserves the futuristic view; as in the other Gospels, it speaks of the coming of Christ, the resurrection of the dead, a final judgment, and life in a future, eternal kingdom (John 5:25, 28-29; 6:27, 39, 40b, 44, 54b; 12:48; 21:22-23). So it has what is commonly called a "future eschatology." On the other hand, it sets forth a "present eschatology" as well, in which it is said that those who believe in Jesus have eternal life already (3:36; 5:24; 6:40a, 47, 54a; 10:28; 17:2-3). Jesus says, "Anyone who hears my word and believes him who sent me has eternal life, and does not come under judgment, but has passed from death to life" (5:24).

In these and other ways it can be said that eschatology is a major ingredient of New Testament thought. There is little doubt about that. The issue that is debated is whether Jesus of Nazareth can be thought to have had an eschatological worldview. The two sides of the debate have been pressed with great force over the decades, and the debate has intensified in recent years.

II. An Eschatological Jesus

The person who gets credit for formulating and popularizing the first credible picture of Jesus as an eschatological prophet is the German New Testament scholar, Johannes Weiss (1863-1914). In a small book of some 67 pages, published in 1892, Weiss set out to make clear what he called "the completely apocalyptic and eschatological character of Jesus' idea of the Kingdom."[8] By "apocalyptic" he meant those fea-

---

8. Johannes Weiss, *Jesus' Proclamation of the Kingdom of God* (Philadelphia: Fortress Press, 1971), p. 56.

tures of Jesus' proclamation that refer to a coming universal destruction of the present world, final judgment, annihilation of the condemned, and eternal bliss for those who will be saved.[9]

Weiss reacted strongly against the views of German liberal theology of his day, including those of his father-in-law, Albrecht Ritschl (1822-89), who had died three years before the publication of the book by Weiss. For Ritschl and others of the time, the Christian religion was concerned primarily with religious experience, of which Jesus was the great teacher and exemplar. When Jesus spoke of the kingdom of God, they thought, he was speaking of something "subjective, inward, or spiritual,"[10] or a "supreme ethical ideal" within a human community on earth.[11]

Against such views, and trying his best to grasp and lay bare the historical meaning of the terminology, Weiss argued on exegetical grounds a different view. He said this:

> the Kingdom of God is a radically superworldly entity which stands in diametric opposition to this world. This is to say that there *can* be no talk of an *innerworldly* development of the Kingdom of God in the mind of Jesus![12]

Weiss summarizes his views about Jesus' eschatology in a number of points, of which the most important are these: (1) Jesus sensed the imminence of the kingdom of God, and even declared that it was dawning; (2) no one, except God himself, can bring the kingdom about; and (3) when the kingdom comes in its fullness, God will destroy this old world, which the devil seeks to rule, and will create a new world.[13] In conclusion, Weiss wrote:

> The Kingdom of God as Jesus thought of it . . . is always the objective messianic Kingdom, which usually is pictured as a territory into which one enters, or as a land in which one has a share, or as a treasure which comes down from heaven.[14]

9. Weiss, *Jesus' Proclamation*, pp. 92-104.

10. Weiss, *Jesus' Proclamation*, p. 133.

11. Weiss, *Jesus' Proclamation*, p. 132, citing Julius Kaftan.

12. Weiss, *Jesus' Proclamation*, p. 114; italics are in the text quoted.

13. Weiss, *Jesus' Proclamation*, pp. 129-31. On p. 91 Weiss writes: "The end is to occur sometime within the important period of the next ten, twenty, or thirty years."

14. Weiss, *Jesus' Proclamation*, p. 133.

Johannes Weiss, by means of his little book at the close of the nineteenth century, set the agenda up to the present not only for understanding the concept of the kingdom of God in the preaching of Jesus, but also for understanding the general tenor of the mission and message of Jesus as a whole. That has been the case especially in German New Testament scholarship. Albert Schweitzer was one of the first to grasp the significance of the work of Weiss and to popularize it at the outset of the twentieth century.[15] Moreover, the views of Weiss came to be widespread by the middle of the twentieth century with Rudolf Bultmann and his followers. Bultmann praised Weiss, saying that his views concerning the proclamation of Jesus have "prevailed triumphantly" over those of his critics.[16] Then too the opening sentences in Bultmann's *Theology of the New Testament*, first published in 1948, concerning Jesus' message echo the views of Weiss:

> The dominant concept of Jesus' message is the *Kingdom of God*. Jesus proclaims its immediately impending irruption, now already making itself felt. The kingdom of God is an eschatological concept. It means the regime of God which will destroy the present course of the world, wipe out all the contra-divine, Satanic power under which the present world groans — and thereby, terminating all pain and sorrow, bring in salvation for the People of God which awaits the fulfillment of the prophets' promises. The coming of the kingdom of God is a miraculous event, which will be brought about by God alone without the help of men.[17]

In a sense, however, what Bultmann gave with one hand, he took back with the other in his hermeneutical program of demythologizing. In that program, he looked for a "deeper meaning" of the mythological preaching of Jesus, and that is "to be open to God's future which is really imminent for every one of us."[18]

---

15. Albert Schweitzer, *The Quest of the Historical Jesus* (New York: Macmillan, 1961), pp. 238-39 (German original: 1906).

16. Rudolf Bultmann, "Foreword" to J. Weiss, *Jesus' Proclamation*, p. vii (published with the 1964 German edition).

17. Rudolf Bultmann, *Theology of the New Testament*, 2 vols. (New York: Charles Scribner's Sons, 1951-55), vol. 1, p. 4. I have substituted, for the sake of consistency, "kingdom of God" for "reign of God" used in this translation — a choice of the translator. In the German text the Greek term (*basileia tou theou*) is used, plus "Gottes-herrschaft."

18. Rudolf Bultmann, *Jesus Christ and Mythology* (New York: Charles Scribner's Sons, 1958), p. 31.

A momentary but highly significant challenge to the view that Jesus was a prophet of an eschatological kingdom was heard from a British contemporary of Bultmann, C. H. Dodd, in his work on the parables of Jesus first published in 1935. Dodd coined a new term, which he called "realized eschatology." He maintained that when Jesus proclaimed the kingdom, he was not speaking of a future reality, but of a power at work in the present. As Dodd himself put it: "The *eschaton* has moved from the future to the present, from the sphere of expectation into that of realized experience"; the proclamation of the kingdom "represents the ministry of Jesus as 'realized eschatology,' that is to say the impact upon this world of the 'powers of the world to come' in a series of events, unprecedented and unrepeatable, now in actual process"[19] centered in the words and deeds of Jesus. Dodd is explicit in saying that, for Jesus, the kingdom is not a future reality to be consummated;[20] it is a reality present already in his ministry. To be sure, God's kingdom is transcendent above this world in heaven as well, but it is not a future reality that is on its way to transform the present. Any interpretation of the kingdom as a future reality must be credited to the account of early Christian proclamation, not to Jesus.[21]

Dodd's viewpoint did not carry the day in the works of major scholars who were his contemporaries or who came after him. But he had posed a challenge that could not be ignored. The result was that major scholars began to see the possibility of an already/not yet schema in the preaching of Jesus. That is to say, the kingdom of God was a present reality in the words and deeds of Jesus, as Dodd insisted, but the kingdom was also a future expectation awaiting its consummation, as in the work of Weiss and his successors. That is the viewpoint argued in the works of scholars such as Joachim Jeremias, Werner Kümmel, and Günther Bornkamm in Germany and Norman Perrin in the United States.[22] Each of these, in his own way, preserved

---

19. C. H. Dodd, *The Parables of the Kingdom*, rev. ed. (New York: Charles Scribner's Sons, 1961), pp. 34-35; cf. pp. 142-43.

20. Dodd, *The Parables of the Kingdom*, pp. 155-56.

21. Dodd, *The Parables of the Kingdom*, pp. 35-36.

22. Joachim Jeremias, *The Parables of Jesus*, 2nd ed. (Upper Saddle River, N.J.: Prentice-Hall, 1972), p. 230; Werner G. Kümmel, *Promise and Fulfilment*, Studies in Biblical Theology 23 (Naperville, Ill.: Allenson, 1957); Günther Bornkamm, *Jesus of Nazareth* (New York: Harper & Brothers, 1960), pp. 64-69; and Norman Perrin, *Rediscovering the Teaching of Jesus* (New York: Harper & Row, 1967), pp. 54-108.

an eschatological Jesus in his rendition of the kingdom in Jesus' proclamation.

Here one can take Bornkamm's *Jesus of Nazareth* as representative. For Bornkamm, the kingdom in the proclamation of Jesus means, on the one hand, "God's future and victory, overcoming the powers of the devil, a shift from this aeon to the next." Jesus' message, he says, is "closely allied to the apocalyptic, cosmic expectations of his day."[23] But on the other hand, already in his ministry Jesus could speak of the kingdom as present: "Jesus' preaching and works are the signs and announcement of the coming kingdom of God."[24] In a useful metaphor, Bornkamm could say that the kingdom is dawning in the ministry of Jesus,[25] but its fulfillment lies in the future, beyond the present course of history. When pressed to speak of Jesus' vocation, Bornkamm's verdict was that Jesus was primarily "a prophet of the coming kingdom of God."[26]

The legacy of those who discerned an eschatological Jesus earlier in the twentieth century continues into the present generation of New Testament scholars. These include such varied persons as E. P. Sanders, John Meier, N. T. Wright, Jürgen Becker,[27] and others too many to name. The work of Sanders may be taken up as an example. For Sanders, Jesus was unmistakably an eschatological prophet. Sanders examines not only the words of Jesus, but also his deeds, to come up with a credible picture of Jesus. Front and center are the words of Jesus concerning the destruction of the Jerusalem temple and his symbolic action within it. For Sanders, Jesus' words and deeds symbolized the coming destruction of the temple,[28] after which there would come a new and perfect temple, given by God, from heaven.[29]

---

23. Bornkamm, *Jesus of Nazareth*, p. 66.

24. Bornkamm, *Jesus of Nazareth*, p. 68.

25. Bornkamm, *Jesus of Nazareth*, pp. 90-95.

26. Bornkamm, *Jesus of Nazareth*, p. 54. On p. 57 Bornkamm also speaks of Jesus as a rabbi, but then he goes on to distinguish him from the usual rabbinic modes of teaching.

27. E. P. Sanders, *Jesus and Judaism* (Philadelphia: Fortress Press, 1985); John P. Meier, *A Marginal Jew*, 2 vols. (New York: Doubleday, 1991-94), vol. 2, p. 331 (a third volume is planned); N. T. Wright, *Jesus and the Victory of God* (Minneapolis: Fortress Press, 1996), pp. 467-74 *et passim*; Jürgen Becker, *Jesus of Nazareth* (New York: Walter de Gruyter, 1998), pp. 186-224.

28. Sanders, *Jesus and Judaism*, p. 90.

29. Sanders, *Jesus and Judaism*, pp. 75-76.

Jesus stood within the tradition of what Sanders calls "Jewish restoration eschatology"; he believed in the coming of the kingdom of God in the near future[30] — a kingdom that would come about by God's own design and that can be designated "otherworldly."[31] What can be said with certainty about Jesus, says Sanders, is that he saw himself as God's last messenger before the establishment of the kingdom. He looked for a new order, the kingdom of God, created by a mighty act of God, in which Jesus and his disciples — together with the poor, meek, and lowly — would have the leading role.[32]

Other works of our time could be included along with those already cited,[33] but perhaps enough has been said already to show that the picture of Jesus as a prophet, even an eschatological prophet, has captured the imagination of major interpreters right up to the present. But now we should turn to another major way of portraying Jesus of Nazareth.

III. A Non-Eschatological Jesus

Shortly after Johannes Weiss promoted the view of Jesus as an eschatological prophet, the famous church historian of Berlin, Adolf von Harnack, sought to provide a view of Jesus that he thought was more credible and useful for proclamation in the church. During the academic year of 1899-1900 he gave a series of sixteen lectures to some six hundred students from all departments within the University of Berlin on the topic, "What Is Christianity?" The lectures were given without manuscript or even notes, but an enthusiastic listener took them down in shorthand, and within a year they were published widely in Germany and then in English translation in England and America.[34]

---

30. Sanders, *Jesus and Judaism*, pp. 155-56, 170-73, 237-39, 319, 321, 326, 330, 335, 340.

31. Sanders, *Jesus and Judaism*, pp. 142, 236.

32. Sanders, *Jesus and Judaism*, p. 319.

33. These include, for example, Richard H. Hiers, *The Historical Jesus and the Kingdom of God: Present and Future in the Message and Ministry of Jesus*, University of Florida Monograph Series 38 (Gainesville: University of Florida, 1973); Hans Conzelmann, *Jesus* (Philadelphia: Fortress Press, 1973), pp. 68-81; A. E. Harvey, *Jesus and the Constraints of History* (Philadelphia: Westminster Press, 1982), pp. 86-90; and Bart D. Ehrman, *Jesus, Apocalyptic Prophet of the New Millennium* (New York: Oxford University Press, 1999).

34. Adolf von Harnack, *What Is Christianity?* (New York: G. P. Putnam's Sons, 1901).

In these lectures Harnack recognized that Jesus proclaimed a message of the coming kingdom of God, which would be a "future event," an "objective" and "external" reality, which Jesus described in colorful, apocalyptic terms. But Harnack claimed that, in speaking this way, Jesus simply used the traditional language and imagery of his day. The true greatness of Jesus was what *distinguished* him from his contemporaries. Specifically, Jesus spoke of the kingdom as "something inward [within the human soul], something which is already present and making its entrance at the moment." All the apocalyptic imagery, claimed Harnack, was the outer husk of an essential kernel; it was the traditional language, but it held within it a true and deeper meaning.[35] In an eloquent fashion Harnack summarized as follows:

> If anyone wants to know what the kingdom of God and the coming of it meant in Jesus' message, he must read and study his parables. He will then see what it is that is meant. The kingdom of God comes by coming to the individual, by entering into his soul and laying hold of it. True, the kingdom of God is the rule of God; but it is the rule of the holy God in the hearts of individuals; *it is God himself in his power.* From this point of view everything that is dramatic in the external and historical sense has vanished; and gone, too, are all the external hopes for the future. Take whatever parable you will, the parable of the sower, of the pearl of great price, of the treasure buried in the field — the word of God, God himself, is the kingdom. It is not a question of angels and devils, thrones and principalities, but of God and the soul, the soul and its God.[36]

Harnack's lectures on "What Is Christianity?" can be considered one of the most lucid statements of German liberal theology of that era. And although one might smile at the perspective Harnack offered on the Christian faith, one can still hear echoes of his views today from many a pulpit.

In our own time there is a new impetus to move away from the picture of Jesus as an eschatological prophet. That impetus is being led by persons such as Marcus Borg, Burton Mack, John Dominic Crossan, Robert Funk, and the Fellows of the Jesus Seminar. One could begin this part of the presentation with any of these. It is proba-

---

35. Harnack, *What Is Christianity?* pp. 52-56.
36. Harnack, *What Is Christianity?* p. 56.

bly best to begin with one of the best known and most forthright of this group, and that is Marcus Borg.

In a series of books and articles,[37] Borg has challenged the conventional picture of Jesus as an eschatological prophet. He urges that we dismiss an eschatological understanding of Jesus,[38] saying that it is "mistaken and misleading."[39] He calls for a thorough spring housecleaning, tossing the legacy of Johannes Weiss into the dumpster. He says explicitly that "there is no significant exegetical basis for the eschatological Jesus."[40] Instead, Borg maintains, we should understand Jesus as deeply involved with the social world of his time and place rather than with otherworldly matters.[41] Jesus, says Borg, was both deeply spiritual and deeply political.[42] At the center of his proclamation was the kingdom of God. But we ought to understand that term symbolically. The term, Borg says, "symbolized the experience of God, the vision of God which transformed existence";[43] it is not a term that points to a temporally conceived future.[44] In a crisp summary, Borg puts it this way:

> For Jesus, the language of the kingdom was a way of speaking of the power of the Spirit and the new life which it created. The coming of the kingdom is the coming of the Spirit, both into individual lives and into history itself. Entering the Kingdom is entering the life of the Spirit, being drawn into the "way" which Jesus taught and was. That Kingdom has an existence within history as the alternative community of Jesus, that community which lives the life of the Spirit. That

37. Among them are the following: Marcus J. Borg, *Conflict, Holiness and Politics in the Teachings of Jesus* (New York: Edwin Mellen, 1984); *Jesus: A New Vision* (San Francisco: Harper & Row, 1987); *Meeting Jesus Again for the First Time* (San Francisco: Harper & Row, 1993); "A Temperate Case for a Noneschatological Jesus," *Foundations and Facets Forum* 2, no. 3 (September 1986): 81-102; "Portraits of Jesus in Contemporary North American Scholarship," *Harvard Theological Review* 84 (1991): 1-22; "Jesus and Eschatology: A Reassessment," *Images of Jesus Today*, ed. James H. Charlesworth and Walter P. Weaver (Valley Forge, Pa.: Trinity Press International, 1994), pp. 42-67; and *Jesus in Contemporary Scholarship* (Valley Forge, Pa.: Trinity Press International, 1994).

38. M. Borg, *Jesus: A New Vision*, pp. 10-14; "A Temperate Case for a Noneschatological Jesus," pp. 86, 95; and "Portraits of Jesus," p. 13.

39. M. Borg, "Portraits of Jesus," p. 14.

40. M. Borg, "A Temperate Case for a Noneschatological Jesus," p. 95.

41. M. Borg, "Portraits of Jesus," p. 14.

42. M. Borg, *Jesus: A New Vision*, p. x.

43. M. Borg, *Conflict*, p. 261.

44. M. Borg, *Conflict*, p. 260.

Kingdom is also something to be hoped for, to be brought about by the power or Spirit of God. Life in the Spirit is thus life lived in relationship to the kingly power of God. Indeed, life in the Spirit is life in the Kingdom of God.[45]

From that understanding of the essential thrust of the message of Jesus, Borg goes on to commend it to the church and the wider culture as a challenge. Jesus, he says, calls people away from the life of "conventional wisdom" and "points us to human community and history, to an alternative culture which seeks to make the world more compassionate."[46] It is Borg's judgment that such a picture of Jesus makes sense in two ways: it makes sense of the gospel record, and it makes sense for our own understanding of reality.[47]

In addition to Borg, a number of other North American scholars are portraying Jesus as a proclaimer of a non-eschatological kingdom. The adjective "North American" is important here, since the phenomenon does not seem to be appearing in Europe. What is happening is that, according to these scholars, Jesus was not an eschatological prophet as heretofore sketched, but a non-eschatological sage.

There can be no doubt whether or not Jesus was in some way a sage. By the estimate of one scholar, Charles Carlston, the Synoptic Gospels contain about 102 wisdom sayings attributed to Jesus.[48] John Dominic Crossan has devoted an entire book to the aphorisms of Jesus — mostly wisdom sayings — and his list of such sayings amounts to 133.[49] The sheer number of such sayings must convince all but the most extreme skeptic that Jesus was a wisdom teacher, a sage.[50]

It is important to recognize that wisdom sayings of Jesus are found in all the main tributaries of the Synoptic tradition. They are

45. M. Borg, *Jesus: A New Vision*, pp. 198-99.

46. M. Borg, *Jesus: A New Vision*, p. 199.

47. M. Borg, *Jesus: A New Vision*, p. x.

48. Charles E. Carlston, "Proverbs, Maxims, and the Historical Jesus," *Journal of Biblical Literature* 99 (1980): 91.

49. John Dominic Crossan, *In Fragments: The Aphorisms of Jesus* (San Francisco: Harper & Row, 1983).

50. Cf. also William A. Beardslee, "The Wisdom Tradition and the Synoptic Gospels," *Journal of the American Academy of Religion* 35 (1967): 231-40; James M. Robinson, "Jesus as Sophos and Sophia: Wisdom Tradition and the Gospels," *Aspects of Wisdom in Judaism and Early Christianity*, ed. Robert L. Wilken (Notre Dame, Ind.: University of Notre Dame Press, 1975), pp. 1-16; and Leo G. Perdue, "The Wisdom Sayings of Jesus," *Foundations and Facets Forum* 2, no. 3 (September 1986): 3-35.

particularly abundant in the so-called Q material — some 225 verses of mostly sayings material common to Matthew and Luke, not derived from Mark. But wisdom sayings are also scattered about in the Gospel of Mark and the special traditions known to Matthew and Luke.[51] This observation invites us to understand Jesus as a teacher engaged in the creation and transmission of wisdom sayings. And so we hear Jesus say, for example, "It is easier for a camel to go through the eye of a needle than for someone who is rich to enter the kingdom of God" (Mark 10:25//Matt. 19:24//Luke 18:25).

The hypothetical Q document has taken on renewed importance for those who are contending for a non-eschatological Jesus. The very existence of Q continues to be challenged by a few scholars,[52] but studies of Q go on unabated nevertheless.[53] Since it is thought that the Q document originated in the middle of the first century in Palestine or Syria — in other words, close to the time and places of the ministry of Jesus of Nazareth — the sayings in Q are taken as prime materials for reconstructing the teachings of Jesus.

In older works on the Synoptic Gospels, Q was posited simply as a document behind the Gospels of Matthew and Luke. But Q studies entered a new stage some time ago. People routinely speak of a Q community. If there was a Q document, there had to be a Q community to produce it. This shift began sometime after World War II, and from that time on major interpreters such as T. W. Manson, Werner Kümmel, and Heinz Tödt suggested that the Q document was composed within a community for whom the preaching of the cross and resurrection was a presupposition for its existence.[54] (Q has no narra-

---

51. Cf. L. Perdue, "The Wisdom Sayings of Jesus," p. 32.

52. Cf. Michael D. Goulder, "Is Q a Juggernaut?" *Journal of Biblical Literature* 115 (1996): 667-81; and *Beyond the Q Impasse — Luke's Use of Matthew: A Demonstration by the Research Team of the International Institute for Gospel Studies,* ed. Allan J. McNicol with David L. Dungan and David B. Peabody (Valley Forge, Pa.: Trinity Press International, 1996).

53. A major volume in this area is *The Gospel Behind the Gospels: Current Studies on Q,* ed. Ronald A. Piper, Novum Testamentum Supplement 75 (Leiden: E. J. Brill, 1995), including the opening essay by R. A. Piper, "In Quest of Q: The Direction of Q Studies," pp. 1-18.

54. T. W. Manson, *The Sayings of Jesus* (London: SCM Press, 1949), pp. 13-17; Heinz T. Tödt, *The Son of Man in the Synoptic Tradition* (Philadelphia: Westminster Press, 1965), p. 250; Werner G. Kümmel, *Introduction to the New Testament,* rev. ed. (Nashville: Abingdon, 1975), p. 74; Leonhard Goppelt, *Theology of the New Testament,* 2 vols. (Grand

tive of the cross and resurrection, but these persons claimed that the cross and resurrection were presupposed by it.) But now all that has changed. John Kloppenborg has proposed that Q is a layered document, consisting of three distinguishable layers or strata. Its earliest recension can be attributed to a band of followers of Jesus who treasured his wisdom sayings and placed no emphasis whatsoever on his crucifixion, death, and resurrection. The apocalyptic material within Q as we now know it must be considered additional material imposed on the earlier non-apocalyptic layer. Finally, as one untimely born, the narrative of the Temptation of Jesus was added at the third stage of development.[55] For Kloppenborg, these three things — wisdom, apocalyptic, and narrative — could not have existed from the beginning in one document. They represent three separate strata, one imposed upon the other. The concept of Q as a layered document has been endorsed by a number of scholars, such as Helmut Koester, Burton Mack, John Dominic Crossan, and others.[56] And the corollary drawn from that hypothesis is that the earliest layer is most in touch with who Jesus was, a wisdom teacher, not a proclaimer of an eschatological kingdom.

The picture of Jesus as a sage has been enhanced not only by the new view concerning a stratified Q and an early non-eschatological Q community, but also by the discovery of the full text of the *Gospel of Thomas* at Nag Hammadi, Egypt, in 1945.[57] That document contains 114 sayings of Jesus, many of which are wisdom sayings. Moreover, there are scholars now who argue that the *Gospel of Thomas* may not have been composed in the mid-second century, as usually thought,[58]

Rapids: Eerdmans, 1981-82), vol. 1, p. 5; and Marinus de Jonge, *Christology in Context: The Earliest Christian Response to Jesus* (Philadelphia: Westminster Press, 1988), pp. 83-84.

55. John Kloppenborg, *The Formation of Q: Trajectories in Ancient Wisdom Collections* (Philadelphia: Fortress Press, 1987); Burton L. Mack, *The Lost Gospel: The Book of Q and Christian Origins* (San Francisco: HarperCollins, 1993), pp. 35-39.

56. Helmut Koester, *Ancient Christian Gospels: Their History and Development* (Philadelphia: Trinity Press International, 1990), pp. 133-49; B. Mack, *The Lost Gospel*, pp. 71-102; and John Dominic Crossan, *The Birth of Christianity* (San Francisco: HarperCollins, 1998), pp. 250-52. For surveys of still other scholars, cf. Christopher Tuckett, *Q and the History of Early Christianity: Studies on Q* (Edinburgh: T. & T. Clark, 1996), pp. 41-82.

57. English translations of the *Gospel of Thomas* have been published many times, such as in *The Nag Hammadi Library in English*, ed. James M. Robinson, 3rd ed. (San Francisco: HarperCollins, 1988), pp. 124-38.

58. Among others, the following can be mentioned: Charles-Henri Puech, "Gnostic Gospels and Related Documents," *New Testament Apocrypha,* ed. Edgar Hennecke and

but in the first.[59] Indeed, it has been suggested in a jointly authored essay by Helmut Koester and Stephen Patterson that much of the material in the *Gospel of Thomas* may have been written as early as the 30s or 40s of the first century,[60] and in the book from the Jesus Seminar called *The Five Gospels* it is said that the first edition of the *Gospel of Thomas* was probably composed during the decade of the 50s.[61] In either case, the *Gospel of Thomas* — or at least portions of it — would antedate any of the canonical Gospels.[62] The impact of all this is to suggest that the wisdom sayings, especially of Q and the *Gospel of Thomas*, preserve for us the authentic Jesus, Jesus the sage.

In keeping with the renewed importance of Q studies and the new interest in the *Gospel of Thomas*, several scholars of our time have proposed a portrait of Jesus the sage. John Dominic Crossan, for example, speaks of Jesus as a "peasant Jewish Cynic," who by his healing, miracles, and parables brought individuals into an unmediated contact with God and one another.[63] But Jesus the peasant Jewish Cynic resembles Jesus the sage. According to Crossan, Jesus did indeed teach

---

Wilhelm Schneemelcher, 2 vols. (Philadelphia: Westminster Press, 1963-65), vol. 1, p. 305; R. McL. Wilson, *Studies in the Gospel of Thomas* (London: A. R. Mowbray, 1960), pp. 7-8; Bertil Gärtner, *The Theology of the Gospel According to Thomas* (New York: Harper & Brothers, 1961), p. 271; Johannes Leipoldt, *Das Evangelium nach Thomas: Koptisch und Deutsch*, Texte und Untersuchungen 101 (Berlin: Akademie, 1967), p. 17; Jacques-É. Ménard, *L'Évangile selon Thomas*, Nag Hammadi Studies 5 (Leiden: E. J. Brill, 1975), p. 3; Klyne R. Snodgrass, "The Gospel of Thomas: A Second Century Gospel," *Second Century* 7 (1989-90): 19-38; Michael Fieger, *Das Thomasevangelium: Einleitung, Kommentar, und Systematik*, Neutestamentliche Abhandlungen 22 (Münster: Aschendorff, 1991), pp. 4, 7; and Beate Blatz, "The Coptic Gospel of Thomas," *New Testament Apocrypha*, rev. ed., ed. Wilhelm Schneemelcher, 2 vols. (Louisville: Westminster/John Knox, 1991-92), vol. 1, p. 113.

59. Helmut Koester, *Introduction to the New Testament*, 2 vols. (Philadelphia: Fortress Press, 1982), vol. 2, p. 152; Koester, *Ancient Christian Gospels*, pp. 21, 84; Stevan Davies, *The Gospel of Thomas and Christian Wisdom* (New York: Seabury, 1983), p. 3; and Ron Cameron, *The Other Gospels: Non-Canonical Gospel Texts* (Philadelphia: Westminster Press, 1982), p. 25.

60. Helmut Koester and Stephen J. Patterson, "The Gospel of Thomas: Does It Contain Authentic Sayings of Jesus?" *Bible Review* 6, no. 2 (April 1990): 37. Cf. also S. Davies, *The Gospel of Thomas*, p. 3, who places the completed work in the era 50-70 C.E..

61. Robert W. Funk et al., *The Five Gospels: The Search for the Authentic Words of Jesus* (New York: Macmillan, 1993), pp. 474, 548.

62. Some reasons for rejecting such a view are set forth in Arland J. Hultgren, *The Rise of Normative Christianity* (Minneapolis: Fortress Press, 1994), pp. 58-61.

63. John Dominic Crossan, *The Historical Jesus: The Life of a Mediterranean Jewish Peasant* (San Francisco: HarperCollins, 1991), pp. 421-22.

an eschatological message, but it was a "sapiential eschatology," not an apocalyptic one. "*Sapiential eschatology* emphasizes the *sapientia* (Latin for 'wisdom') of knowing how to live here and now today so that God's present power is forcibly evident to all."[64]

A person who provides one of the most robust pictures of Jesus the sage is Burton Mack. Mack is the author of two books about Christian origins,[65] and in them he makes claims about the under-standing of Jesus that his first followers had. Mack asserts that there were "Jesus movements" prior to and alongside of what we can properly call early Christianity, and he suggests that these move-ments preserved a better memory of who Jesus was than the early Christians did. Those who were actual Christians gave too much weight to the so-called Christ-myth — the story of God's redemp-tive work in Christ through his death and resurrection — and they suppressed the living memory of Jesus as he actually was. It is to the early "Jesus people," not the early "Christians," that we should look for information about Jesus. And the place to find the legacy of Jesus is in the Q material, for the people of Q, he says, were Jesus people, not Christians.[66] In a rather chilling statement, Mack says: "The nar-rative gospels" — by which he means Matthew, Mark, and Luke — "can no longer be viewed as trustworthy accounts of unique and stu-pendous historical events at the foundation of the Christian faith. The gospels must now be seen as the result of early Christian myth-making."[67] Or again, he says forthrightly that "the narrative gospels have no claim as historical accounts. The gospels are imaginative creations."[68]

Mack dismisses the views of Johannes Weiss explicitly, saying that the teachings of Jesus are classified better under the category of wis-dom than apocalyptic.[69] He brings to the fore the importance of the Q

---

64. John D. Crossan, *The Essential Jesus: Original Sayings and Earliest Images* (San Francisco: HarperCollins, 1994), p. 8.

65. Burton L. Mack, *A Myth of Innocence: Mark and Christian Origins* (Philadelphia: Fortress Press, 1988); and *The Lost Gospel: The Book of Q and Christian Origins* (San Fran-cisco: HarperCollins, 1993). Cf. also Burton L. Mack, "The Christ and Jewish Wisdom," *The Messiah: Developments in Earliest Judaism and Christianity,* ed. James H. Charlesworth (Minneapolis: Fortress Press, 1992), pp. 192-221.

66. B. Mack, *The Lost Gospel,* p. 5.

67. B. Mack, *The Lost Gospel,* p. 10.

68. B. Mack, *The Lost Gospel,* p. 247.

69. B. Mack, *The Lost Gospel,* pp. 30-31.

material, the *Gospel of Thomas,* and recent studies of the parables of Jesus to argue that Jesus was remembered first of all by his followers as a teacher of wisdom, not as a prophet, and certainly not as an apocalyptic prophet.[70] The picture that Mack comes up with is Jesus as a sage in the asocial, iconoclastic tradition of the ancient cynics.[71]

Out of his work, Mack sketches some of its relevance for modern Christians. He argues that at the beginning of Christianity a lot of mythmaking went on that has been dangerous to the world's health, especially the mandate to convert the world exclusively to Christianity[72] — apparently something that Jesus and his followers would not have had in mind. The wisdom tradition spelled out in the Q material, he writes, provides for us a different and better way to go. As he puts it near the end of his book on Q, we have in the Q tradition a limited number of truths and symbols. "A few proverbs, maxims, and memorable figures can offer guidance even in the midst of confusing times. The people of Q coined a few injunctions that still work as golden rules for many Christians: 'Love your enemies' and 'Turn the other cheek.'"[73] There we have enough for a new social vision.

There are others, besides those already mentioned, who have portrayed Jesus as sage.[74] Jesus as sage, for example, is the dominant understanding of Jesus that has emerged out of the Jesus Seminar. In the Introduction to the published results of the Seminar in *The Five Gospels,* Robert Funk writes that Jesus should be thought of as a "traveling sage" or simply a "sage,"[75] and his message was non-eschatological.[76] According to Funk, an eschatological Jesus reigned from the time of Weiss and Schweitzer to the end of World War II. But, he says, evidence for such a view has eroded, and since then a non-eschatological Jesus is one of the pillars of New Testament scholarship.[77] As a consequence, any passages in the Gospels that have an eschatological,

70. B. Mack, *The Lost Gospel,* pp. 34-39.

71. This apt description of Mack's Jesus is borrowed from Pheme Perkins, "Jesus Before Christianity: Cynic and Sage?" *Christian Century* 110, no. 22 (July 28–Aug. 4, 1993): 749.

72. Perkins, "Jesus Before Christianity," p. 255.

73. Perkins, "Jesus Before Christianity," p. 257.

74. For a survey, cf. Ben Witherington, *Jesus the Sage: The Pilgrimage of Wisdom* (Minneapolis: Fortress Press, 1994).

75. R. Funk, *The Five Gospels,* pp. 1, 27, 32, 33.

76. R. Funk, *The Five Gospels,* p. 4.

77. R. Funk, *The Five Gospels,* pp. 3-4.

and especially apocalyptic, content are considered additions to the Jesus tradition, not from Jesus himself.

IV. Observations and Critique

How shall one evaluate the present situation, in which there are strong arguments on each side of the question of an eschatological or non-eschatological Jesus? Five points follow.

1. We begin with a question. Can one posit the existence of a Q community that treasured the wisdom sayings of Jesus apart from cross, resurrection, and apocalyptic? The only way to do so is to reconstruct an early version of Q that fits the proposal — an early hypothetical layer of a hypothetical document that was sapiential and in no way apocalyptic. To go even further, one has to posit that once upon a time there was a hypothetical theology that we can now observe in a hypothetical layer of a hypothetical document produced by a hypothetical community. Furthermore, one must assume that that community, the Q community, was a cell group walled off from other Christian traditions and communities, that it never reflected on the meaning of Jesus' death and resurrection, and that the reconstructed document contained all that the Q people ever thought important about Jesus. But all that is totally arbitrary. By analogy one could apply the same viewpoint to the Epistle of James. Since the Epistle of James mentions neither the cross nor the resurrection, and contains a great deal of wisdom sayings, must we conclude that the author and his community placed no positive evaluation whatsoever on the cross and resurrection of Jesus? Moreover, for all we know, the Q document may have been the work of a solitary figure who had no community to receive what he wrote.

But let us assume that there was indeed a Q community. The view that Q reflects an early form of a Jesus movement that placed no emphasis at all on the cross and resurrection is mistaken. Within the Q document itself, if we do not posit the existence of hypothetical layers, there are allusions to Jesus' rejection, death, exaltation, and coming again as Son of Man to judge the world — the major points of the common Christian kerygma! These allusions can be mentioned briefly: His rejection is alluded to in the sayings that the Son of Man has no place to lay his head (Luke 9:58//Matt. 8:20) and that prophets coming to Jerusalem are always killed (Luke 13:34//Matt. 23:37). His death on the cross is alluded to most strikingly in the saying that a disciple must carry his *own* cross and follow after Jesus (Luke 14:27// Matt. 10:38). His exaltation, reign, and parousia are alluded to in apocalyptic Son of Man sayings (e.g., Luke 12:40//Matt. 24:44; Luke 17:26-30//Matt. 24:37-39). They speak explicitly of his coming again, and since he is to come again, his resurrection and heavenly reign are presupposed. These are also alluded to allegorically in the Parable of the Pounds/Talents, in which a man departs to receive a kingdom and then returns to exercise judgment (Luke 19:12-27//Matt. 25:14-30).

The view of Kloppenborg — with his multilayered, stratified Q — allows him to claim that the earliest form of Q was "genre bound" so as to exclude all thought of the cross and resurrection.[78] And since the document would not have had such thought, neither did the community that produced it.[79] But how do we know that, and how can we be so certain that there was such an early edition?[80] And can one claim, as he and others do, that wisdom and eschatology are incompatible in the initial drafting of a document? Wisdom and eschatology are often bound together in both Jewish and Christian literatures. An example of this in Jewish literature is the Wisdom of Solomon, which extols wisdom but also speaks of divine judgment to come (4:19-20) and eternal life for the righteous (3:4; 5:15-16). An example in Christian literature is 1 Corinthians, in which Paul draws upon wisdom to instruct his hearers in the ways of love in chapter 13 and has an eschatological scenario in chapter 15. Still another example is the Letter of James, the most sapiential book of the New Testament, which also speaks of the parousia of Christ (5:7-8), a final judgment (2:12-13; 3:1; 5:9, 12), and eternal blessedness for the redeemed (1:12; 2:5).

2. The use of the *Gospel of Thomas* as an early source on the teachings of Jesus is also in need of critique. That it was composed already in the

---

78. J. Kloppenborg, *The Formation of Q,* pp. 2, 25.

79. John Kloppenborg, "'Easter Faith' and the Sayings Gospel Q," *The Apocryphal Jesus and Christian Origins: Semeia 49,* ed. Ron Cameron (Atlanta: Scholars Press, 1990), pp. 71, 76, 82, 90; cf. H. Koester, *Ancient Christian Gospels,* p. 160.

80. For critique of Kloppenborg's thesis, cf. Arland D. Jacobson, *The First Gospel: An Introduction to Q* (Sonoma: Polebridge Press, 1992), pp. 50-51; and C. Tuckett, *Q and the History of Early Christianity,* pp. 69-74. That a non-eschatological stage of Q ever existed is challenged by Helmut Koester, "Jesus the Victim," *Journal of Biblical Literature* 111 (1992): 7.

first century C.E. is most unlikely. The earliest textual evidence comes from three small Greek fragments among the Oxyrhynchus Papyri from ca. 200 C.E.,[81] providing the latest possible dating, the *terminus ad quem*. But how early could it have been composed? Its earliest attestation is in the writings of Hippolytus (d. ca. 235 C.E.) and Origen (d. ca. 254 C.E.) sometime in the first half of the third century.[82] Taking the evidence as a whole, the more widely held view that this Gospel was composed sometime in the second half of the second century is more credible.[83]

3. A major question revolves around the meaning of the term "kingdom of God." Scholars of various perspectives have affirmed that the kingdom of God was central or at least prominent in the proclamation of Jesus.[84] The problem is what possible meanings Jesus might have attached to it.

The full range of meanings cannot be rehearsed here. But a few things can be said. Certainly within the concept of the kingdom is the age-old theological affirmation of Israel that God is king, and that God exercises dominion over the world. That theme is expressed above all in the Psalms and the prophets.[85] The problem is that in history and nature there is not enough evidence of God's rule, God's dominion. And so there is the petition of the Lord's Prayer, for example, that God's kingdom might come (Matt. 6:10//Luke 11:3). And eschatological hopes arose among the people of Israel of various sorts — be they

81. Cf. *The Oxyrhynchus Papyri*, ed. Bernard P. Grenfell, Arthur S. Hunt, et al., 31 vols. (London: Egypt Exploration Fund, 1898-1966), vol. 4, p. 1; and Harold W. Attridge, "The Gospel According to Thomas (Greek Fragments)," *Nag Hammadi Codex II, 2-7*, ed. Bentley Layton, Nag Hammadi Studies 20, 2 vols. (Leiden: E. J. Brill, 1989), vol. 1, pp. 96-99. Attridge places POxy 1 "shortly after A.D. 200" (p. 97); POxy 654 "in the middle of the third century" (p. 97); and POxy 655 "between A.D. 200 and 250" (p. 98).

82. Hippolytus, *Refutation of All Heresies* 5.2 (in some editions, 5.7.20); Origen, *Homily on Luke* 1.

83. For details, cf. Arland J. Hultgren, "The Use of Sources in the Quest for Jesus: What You Use Is What You Get," *The Quest for Jesus and the Christian Faith*, ed. Frederick J. Gaiser, Word & World Supplement 3 (St. Paul, Minn.: Luther Seminary, 1997), pp. 34-41.

84. E. P. Sanders, *Jesus*, p. 326; Geza Vermes, *Jesus and the World of Judaism* (Philadelphia: Fortress Press, 1984), p. 32; idem, *The Religion of Jesus the Jew* (Minneapolis: Fortress Press, 1993), p. 120; M. Borg, *Conflict*, pp. 248-49; N. Perrin, *Rediscovering the Teaching of Jesus*, p. 54; John Reumann, *Jesus in the Church's Gospels* (Philadelphia: Fortress Press, 1968), p. 142; R. Funk, *The Five Gospels*, p. 40; and Bruce Chilton, "Introduction," *The Kingdom of God in the Teaching of Jesus*, ed. B. Chilton, Issues in Religion and Theology 5 (Philadelphia: Fortress Press, 1984), p. 1.

85. Some examples include Psalms 103:19; 145:10-13; Isaiah 44:6-8.

Pharisees, Essenes, messianists, or simply people of the land, as documented well in the writings of Josephus and in the Qumran scrolls.[86]

But when and how does that kingdom come? Does it come with apocalyptic drama, as an outer world-transforming event? Or does it come with spiritual force in the hearts of people who seek it? In short, is the primary accent on temporality and final accountability, or is it on present spirituality and empowerment?

Interpreters may never agree on the matter. But in working toward a conclusion, we need to pay attention to the actual metaphors used in the language of Jesus transmitted to us in the Gospels. There we see several major figures of speech, most of them coming to us in all strands of the synoptic tradition and frequently in the *Gospel of Thomas* as well: the kingdom is autonomous, as in the parables of growth;[87] it is something one enters, rather than something that enters into us;[88] it is something that comes upon us;[89] it is a gift, or inheritance, to be received;[90] and occasionally it is spoken of as an eschatological, post-historical reality — and that is so in all strands of the synoptic tradition (Mark, Q, L, and M).[91] In short, the kingdom is not simply something that one experiences inwardly; it is an outer and eternal reality, something greater than the dimensions of our own spiritual potentials in this world. The kingdom in the speech of Jesus exceeds every experience and domain known to anyone, whether temporal, spatial, or spiritual, even if a person apprehends it in part. It is a reality with which one must reckon. So a prophet speaks of it, indeed an eschatological prophet. Spirit terminology, as in the case of Marcus Borg, will not suffice as an equivalent for it.

---

86. Josephus, *Jewish War* 2.8; for a survey and discussion of texts from Qumran, see the chapter on "Eschatology" by Helmer Ringgren, *The Faith of Qumran: Theology of the Dead Sea Scrolls* (Philadelphia: Fortress Press, 1963), pp. 152-98.

87. Cf. the Parables of the Seed Growing Secretly (Mark 4:26-29; *Gos. Thom.* 21), the Mustard Seed (Mark 4:30-32; *Gos. Thom.* 20), and the Leaven (Matt. 13:33, M tradition; *Gos. Thom.* 96).

88. Mark 9:47; 10:23-25; Matt. 5:20; 7:21; 18:3; 21:31 (the latter four are M tradition); *Gos. Thom.* 22, 64. Cf. also John 3:5; Acts 14:22.

89. Mark 9:1; Luke 11:2//Matt. 6:10 (Q); Luke 11:20//Matt. 12:28 (Q); *Gos. Thom.* 49.

90. Mark 10:14-15; Luke 6:20//Matt. 5:3 (Q); Matt. 5:10 (M); 25:34 (M); Luke 12:32 (L). Cf. also 1 Cor. 6:10; 15:50; Gal. 5:21.

91. Mark 14:25; Luke 13:28-29//Matt. 8:11-12 (Q); Matt. 13:43; 16:19; 20:21; 25:34 (M traditions); Luke 14:15; 22:16, 30 (L traditions). Cf. also 1 Cor. 15:24.

4. There is one point at which the non-eschatological interpretation of the kingdom deserves a hearing. The non-eschatological view
seems increasingly satisfactory in our day for certain people. There is
an important point to be made. If it is the case that the eschatological
view is correct, so that in the proclamation of Jesus the kingdom is a
reality that was both present in his words and deeds and as a future
expectation, what can one say of the intervening time, the time in
which we now live? Is the era between Easter and the parousia devoid
of the presence of the kingdom?

The answer to that question is, of course, a resounding no. The
writings of Paul and John speak of the life of the believer as renewed
by the power of the Spirit, the eschatological gift that is effective
proleptically within the church.

I suggest that much of the problem that some have with an eschatological Jesus lies right here. It is actually a theological matter.
Given the rise and power of secularism, on the one hand, and the
popularity of a non-ecclesial spirituality on the other, the stage is set
for a non-eschatological Jesus. That is a Jesus who is available
within one's own private spirituality, a Jesus who has been freed not
only from dogma, but also from the community that receives him in
the breaking of bread within the communion of saints, and a Jesus
of a future kingdom, in which many will come from east and west to
sit at table with Abraham, Isaac, and Jacob in the kingdom of heaven
(Matt. 8:11). We should make no mistake. Behind the picture of a
non-eschatological Jesus is a theological commitment. It is a revital-
ization of a theological perspective in vogue a century ago, calling
for a reinvention of Christianity, so that it is essentially an explication of the teachings of Jesus construed in such a way that the kingdom of God is the power of God or some form of spirituality in the
heart of the individual. That is a religious expression that can do
very well — thank you — without cross, resurrection, parousia, final
judgment, and eternal communion with the risen Lord and those he
has redeemed.

5. While Robert Funk has written that the evidence for an eschatological Jesus has eroded since the middle of the twentieth century,[92]
the opposite is actually the case. The discovery of the Dead Sea Scrolls
has served to underscore that an apocalyptic worldview was common

92. R. Funk, *The Five Gospels*, p. 3.

in Palestine of the first century.[93] Add to that the preaching of John the Baptist, which even members of the Jesus Seminar grant to have been eschatological,[94] the eschatological beliefs of the Pharisees (the dominant theological movement of the day), plus the preaching of the early church — whether Palestinian, Pauline, or otherwise — and it is difficult to believe that Jesus did not maintain an eschatological outlook. The alternative rips him out of his historical context.

Eschatology is ubiquitous in the writings of the New Testament. On that there is no debate. The debate centers around the teachings of Jesus. On this, all investigators can agree also that Jesus was a sage. But was he also an eschatological prophet? To work our way through all that, we need what I call a "criterion of crucifiability" for Jesus.[95] Generally it can be said that sages are persons honored by those around them, and they live a long time. Prophets get killed. And a prophet of the coming reign of divine justice, compassion, final judgment, accountability before God, and the renewal of all things — indeed the very reign of God in its fullness — may well end up being killed.

93. Cf. Birger A. Pearson, "An Exposé of the Jesus Seminar," *dialog* 37 (1998): 30.

94. R. Funk, *The Five Gospels*, pp. 40, 132.

95. I use this term in my essay on "The Use of Sources," p. 46. The term was picked up from the oral presentation of that essay and subsequently used in the final version of the essay by Mary M. Knutson, "The Third Quest for the Historical Jesus: Introduction and Bibliography," *The Quest for Jesus*, ed. F. Gaiser, p. 15.

Law and Eschatology:
A Jewish-Christian Intersection

DAVID NOVAK

1. The Doctrinal Dialectic
Between Judaism and Christianity

One can look at the differences between Judaism and Christianity as being centered on the quintessential question: What is the most correct way to be in faith with the Lord God of Israel? Two more specific questions within this largest question have been over the role of law and the role of eschatology in the life of faith, especially how the two are interrelated. It is usually assumed that Christian notions of law and eschatology have been formulated out of earlier Jewish notions, and that these notions have been subsequently developed in contradistinction to the views of those Jews who refused to see these Christian notions as a legitimate development of traditional Jewish doctrine. Many Christians have assumed that Christianity moved forward while Judaism remained in the past. This, of course, has been the basic assumption of Christian supersessionism. Many Jews have responded to this type of supersessionism by arguing that what Christians consider to be the upward development of Jewish doctrine, Jews consider to be a deviation away from the purity of that doctrine. In other words, they have accepted the notion of the timeless quality of Judaism, only differing from the Christian conclusion from it. So, along these lines one could ask: Is Judaism proto-Christianity or is Christianity quasi-Judaism? Are those Jews, indeed most of the Jews, who have continually refused to become Christians, fixated in past tradition or faithful to its source?

Another assumption of this kind of historiography of doctrine is that Christianity has developed out of Judaism and then beyond Judaism, whereas Judaism developed only up to the point of the Christian schism, and then remained frozen in time, as it were, purposefully oblivious to everything that has happened in the world, especially the Christian world, after that time. The thesis of this paper, though, is that this represents a large misunderstanding of Judaism and, probably, of Christianity as well, by both Christians and Jews. Here I shall try to show that Jewish doctrine, especially on the issue of law and eschatology, has undergone considerable development over the course of history after the Christian schism. Moreover, I shall try to show that some of the development of Jewish doctrine has not been *apart from* but *because of* the claims of Christian doctrine. That is, the doctrinal intersection of Judaism and Christianity has not been a once-and-for-all matter but, rather, something that began in Christianity's self-distinction from Judaism and continued in Judaism's self-distinction from Christianity. One can see this ongoing intersection as dialectical: a constant back and forth, forth and back. Indeed, one can see this process of mutual self-distinction as continual from the beginnings of Christianity until the present day. It is obvious that Christianity would not be what it is without this process of intersection with Judaism. It has been less obvious, though, that Judaism has had to continually distinguish itself from Christianity, and that this process has had a profound effect on the inner development of Jewish doctrine itself. Nowhere has this been more evident than on the issue of law and eschatology.

Christianity emerged out of a Jewish milieu that was obsessed with eschatology. The condition of the Jewish people under alien Roman rule made hope for a radically transformed future a central issue for Jews. It was, to borrow a term from Spinoza, *the* theologico-political question. This hope for such a future (generally called *l'atid la-vo*) had three interrelated components: the hope for the days of the Messiah (*yemot ha-mashiah*), the hope for the resurrection of the dead (*tehiyyat ha-metim*), and the hope for the coming-world (*'olam ha-ba*). Although in medieval Jewish theology there was considerable speculation about how these three components designated three different times or three different realms, it seems that at least in the period of the first century

C.E. there was no such differentiation. They were seen as three aspects of one realm. Indeed, one could say that the "coming-world" emphasizes the temporal nature of the end time: it is a time yet future, not an eternal realm already existent into which the present time is finally included.[1] The resurrection of the dead emphasizes the personal nature of the end time: it is a time when persons, who in biblical anthropology could not be conceived other than embodied, are fully restored to the coming-world.[2] The days of the Messiah emphasize the political nature of the end time: it is a time when a polity, with a king at its head, will be the collective form of the coming-world.[3] That is why God's reign is over a collective entity; it is God's kingship and kingdom (malkut shamayim).[4]

It appears that in this period Pharisaic Jews (out of whose Judaism subsequently came both Christianity and Rabbinic Judaism) believed that when the Messiah comes, he will either be resurrected or resurrect the dead himself in order for the living and the dead to live forever in communion with God their king.[5] On this score, both the books of the New Testament (the earlier literary works) and the Rabbinic Writings (the later literary works) seem to be in accord. The question became, therefore: What is the Messiah to do with the law under whose rule the Jewish people had been living since time immemorial?

Since the New Testament is the earlier text, it seems best to look at some key passages there in order to see, along general lines, just

1. Under the influence of Platonism, there were medieval attempts to view *olam ha-ba* as the eternal realm, unchanged and unchanging, without an end or a beginning. Its temporality is, therefore, only subjective, viz., the time of the death of the justified person, *when* he or she enters that realm. Maimonides was the most important advocate of this view (see *Mishneh Torah*: Repentance 8.8). But the earlier rabbinic view of *olam ha-ba* itself being temporal, with a finite beginning at the end of history ("this world," *olam ha-zeh*) and an infinite extension into the future, was always maintained by many post-rabbinic theologians. See D. Novak, *The Theology of Nahmanides Systematically Presented* (Atlanta: Scholars Press, 1992), pp. 129-30.

2. I know of no better conceptual representation of this theological anthropology than that of Reinhold Niebuhr, *The Nature and Destiny of Man*, vol. 2 (New York: Charles Scribner's Sons, 1964), pp. 295-97.

3. See *Babylonian Talmud* (hereafter "B."): Berakhot 34b re Deut. 15:11.

4. See, e.g., *Midrash Rabbah*: Genesis 98.13 re Gen. 49:18. For the use of *shamayim* (lit. "heaven") as a synonym for God, see A. Marmorstein, *The Old Rabbinic Doctrine of God* (New York: KTAV, 1968), pp. 105-7.

5. See Solomon Schechter, *Some Aspects of Rabbinic Theology* (New York: Macmillan, 1909), pp. 97-115.

how Christian eschatology dealt with the question of the law. We should then try to discover in some rabbinic texts what seem to be the Jewish doctrines out of which these Christian doctrines emerged. Afterwards, we should look at how it seems these same Jewish doctrines were modified and developed in response to what appeared to Jews to have been Christian distortions of them. Finally, I shall speculate a bit about what this intersection with Christianity means for Jewish theology today.

2. The Fulfillment of the Law

In the New Testament the relation of law and eschatology first appears in the Sermon on the Mount. There Jesus says:

> Do not suppose that I have come to eliminate *(katalysai)* the Law and the Prophets. I have not come to eliminate them but to fulfill them *(plērōsai)*. . . . not even one little letter or one superscription shall pass away from the Law until everything has come to be *(panta genētai)*. Whoever would leave off even one of the least *(elachistōn)* of these commandments . . . he is least likely *(elachistos)* to be called into the kingdom of God *(basileia tōn ouranōn)*. . . . I say to you that unless your righteousness *(dikaiosynē)* is greater than that of the Scribes and Pharisees, you will not come into the kingdom of God. (Matt. 5:17-20)

A Jew at the time of Jesus could have very well heard this text to mean the following: The kingdom of God will only come when the righteousness *(tsedaqah)* of the people is sufficient for God to fully complete his rule over Israel, which is when "everything has come to be." That righteousness is the complete response of the Jewish people to God's commandments *(mitsvot)* revealed in the Torah. The Scribes and the Pharisees seem to be those who are most punctilious in their observance of the Torah.[6] But Jesus has come to set an example of greater Torah observance than that of those heretofore recognized as the epitome of piety. Only those who follow Jesus and emulate his piety will be worthy of entrance to the coming kingdom of God. They alone will constitute the "saved remnant of Israel" *(she'erit yisrael)*.[7]

---

6. See E. P. Sanders, *Jesus and Judaism* (London: SCM Press, 1985), pp. 245-69.
7. See B. Yoma 38b re 1 Sam. 2:8.

"Fulfillment" here would mean complete personal observance. But what is not yet clear is whether the observance of the commandments is to be completed in this world now in order to attain the kingdom of God as its due reward, or whether the observance of the commandments will continue in the kingdom of God when and only when full observance will be possible. As we shall see, this has always been a disputed issue in Jewish eschatology.

From what follows later in the Gospel of Matthew, it seems that the observance of the commandments of the Torah is a preparation for the kingdom of God, but when that kingdom is considered to have arrived, the time of the commandments will thereby have passed. The kingdom of God will have arrived when the Messiah makes himself known to Israel. Thus when Pharisees see disciples of Jesus gleaning grain on the Sabbath, and complain to Jesus about this obvious violation of the Sabbath prohibition of work, Jesus adopts two strategies in answering their objection: one strictly legal and the other more eschatological (Matt. 12:1-8). On the legal level, he makes the argument that the disciples were starving and, therefore, the preservation of human life takes precedence over the observance of the Sabbath. Since the time when the Maccabees agreed that not to fight the enemies of Israel on the Sabbath would lead to the wholesale destruction of all those who keep the commandments of God, it became common Jewish (especially Pharisaic) teaching that this mandated dispensation applies even to individual Jews in mortal danger, be that danger from human malice or from natural disaster.[8] Human life takes precedence over the prohibition of work on the Sabbath. Jesus surely knew what he was saying and to whom he was saying it. Nevertheless, all of this is simply hypothetical in the light of the categorical conclusion of this whole episode. There Jesus says, "This is because (gar) the Son of Man is lord (kyrios) of the Sabbath" (Matt. 12:8). In other words, the Messiah has the authority from God to dispense Jews from the observance of any of the commandments. That seems to be an essential privilege of his messiahhood.

From the above answer, one could conclude that this simply means the Messiah eo ipso has the authority to dispense some Jews from the observance of the Sabbath ad hoc, not that the Messiah has

---

8. See 1 Macc. 2:32-42; Josephus, Contra Apionem 2.2 and Antiquities 12.6; also, B. Yoma 85b and parallels. Cf. Mark 2:27 and Luke 6:1-5.

declared the time of the observance of the Sabbath per se to be over forever. His authority could thus be like the authority the Rabbis later ascribed to a true prophet, namely, he (or she) could dispense people from ordinary rules by virtue of his (or her) generally accepted status as a prophet. This is unlike an ordinary Rabbi, who would have to give a specific legal justification for any such dispensation.[9] A Rabbi must speak *ad rem;* a prophet can speak *in personam.* Accordingly, could one see the development of Jesus' argument with the Pharisees moving from the interpretive authority of a Rabbi to the more personal authority of a prophet? Thus, when Jesus begins his argument with the Pharisees over the permissibility or nonpermissibility of what the disciples did on *that* Sabbath, he argues with them on their ground, namely, the common assumption that danger to a life requires violation of the Sabbath when that is the only way to save *that* life. His argument up to that point is one that any Rabbi could make with any other Rabbi. However, the question to ask is whether Jesus' messianic authority is something more than the authority of a prophet. Is his personal authority to dispense people from observance of any of the commandments more than just ad hoc?

The pivotal point in the dispute, however, is when Jesus points out how the service of the Temple itself takes precedence over the observance of the Sabbath. Thus the prohibition of lighting a fire on the Sabbath only applies outside the Temple, "in all your dwellings *(moshvoteikehm)*" (Exod. 35:3); but in the Temple itself "the burnt offering of the Sabbath *('olat shabbat)* is offered on each Sabbath *(beshabbatto)*" (Num. 28:10).[10] After making this point Jesus says, "I say to you that this place *(hode)* is greater than the Temple. But if you had known what this means, 'kindness not sacrifice do I desire' [Hos. 6:6], you would not have condemned the innocent *(anaitous)*" (Matt. 12:6-7). Of course, one can interpret Jesus' intention here to be that one should judge by standards less stringent than those of the strict law. This would be like a prophet offering an ad hoc dispensation, this time retroactively, which is one way of looking at divine forgiveness and atonement of sins. But if this were so, why would it have been

9. See B. Yevamot 90b re Deut. 18:15. Nevertheless, later rabbinic interpretation limited prophetic authority to making ad hoc dispensations from the law (see B. Megillah and parallels re Lev. 27:34). Hence a Sage who interprets God's *perpetual* law could be seen as greater than a prophet (see B. Baba Batra 12b re Ps. 90:12).

10. See B. Shabbat 20a re Exod. 35:3.

preceded by Jesus' very legal argument just before? Accordingly, it might be more accurate to say that his argument here is that a higher form of sanctity takes precedence over a lower form of sanctity and thereby dispenses one from the obligations of that lower form of sanctity.[11] The grace or "kindness" of God is that higher form of sanctity, namely, the response to the authority of the Messiah himself. It is much more than the human tendency to bend the strictness of the law in extenuating circumstances. It is thus much more than the authority of any Rabbi, even more than the authority of any prophet.

In the case of the Temple, that lower form of sanctity is everywhere outside the Temple precincts.[12] The difference is spatial. But in the case of the Messiah, whose time has now come, the difference is temporal. Before the messianic time the commandments were in full force; during the messianic time, which is seen as being now *ad aeternum*, the time of the commandments is over. Keeping the commandments has fulfilled its task in this world, up until the coming-world. Thus the word usually translated as "this place" *(hōde)* can be just as easily translated as "this time" (namely, *kairos*).[13] It is the "when" of the Messiah that now determines the "where" of his rule. Sacred space is no longer confined to the Temple; it is to be extended everywhere. As the end of the Gospel of Matthew indicates, that new "where" is the space-time to be extended "even to the farthest end *(synteleias)* of the world *(aiōnos)*" (Matt. 28:20).

So far we have seen what seems to be a temporal thrust to the New Testament's view of the relation of the law and the end time. The law is in full force until the end time arrives in the person of the Messiah. From that time on the Messiah is the norm and it is his life (and death) that is to be emulated by the faithful. However, one does not emulate Jesus' observance of the specific commandments of the Torah; instead, one emulates Jesus' love of God by accepting Jesus himself as the Christ. At this level, Jesus has "fulfilled" the law finally. Nevertheless, it is still unclear what the essential connection between the law and the end time really is. When the author of the Gospel of Matthew uses the term "fulfill" *(plērōsai)* to describe the law as perfectly observed by Jesus, he is still speaking of Jesus' motivation in

11. See, e.g., *Mishnah* (herafter "M."): Berakhot 3.1.
12. See, e.g., M. Rosh Hashanah 4.1.
13. See *Theological Dictionary of the New Testament*, ed. G. Kittel, trans. G. W. Bromiley (Grand Rapids: Eerdmans, 1965), vol. 3, pp. 459-62.

that observance, not what the law itself is, that is, what its function is in the salvific order of God. Enter Paul.

In speaking of the relation of the law and the eschaton, Paul introduces a different term. He says "For Christ is the end *(telos)* of the law, leading all who have faith into righteousness *(eis dikaiosynēn)*" (Rom. 10:4). *Telos* is a term that already had a long history in Greek thought. It was taken to mean either the temporal end of all things, that which they inevitably become at the conclusion of their days *after* they have departed the world, or it was taken to mean the purpose of human activity *within* the world itself.[14] It seems that Paul understands *telos* in both the temporal and the purposeful senses; indeed, he seems to combine them both into one meaning: the purpose of the observance of the commandments of the Torah *has been* to bring those observers to salvation at the end time. Salvation is being saved from the evils of this world, primarily death, which came into the world because of human sin since the first humans. However, the commandments themselves, according to Paul, could not bring about that salvation because the sinfulness of human nature since the Fall prevents anyone and everyone from the *full* observance of the Torah.[15] (Only Jesus, who was not infected with the sinfulness of human nature, could accomplish that.)

The failure of observance of the law can only be known after Jesus the Christ has appeared as the righteousness of God, faith in *whom* having been the true *telos*, the true intentionality of the law all along. The commandments, then, function as a kind of *via negativa*, clearing the way, as it were, for faith's original and everlasting object. Thus Paul praises the Jews for their general purposefulness in trying to keep God's law, while at the same time indicating that they didn't really know the precise object of that trying. "They have a zeal for God *(zēlon theou)*, but not because of what they know *(ou kata epignōsin)*" (Rom. 10:2). Then, at this point, Paul uses the term "righteousness" as a *double entendre*, meaning one thing in God's case, another in the case of humans. "They try *(zētousin)* to set up their righteousness *(idian dikaiosynē)*, but they do not submit themselves to the righteousness of God" (10:3). Now *dikaiosynē* is the Septuagint's rendition of the He-

---

14. See Aeschylus, *Agamemnon*, 928; Sophocles, *Oedipus Rex* 1527-1530; Herodotus, *Persian Wars* 1.32; Aristotle, *Physics* 194a30 and *Nicomachean Ethics* 1100a10-35.

15. See Romans 8:1-4.

brew *tsedaqah*.[16] *Tsedaqah* primarily means what God does graciously
for humans. Secondarily, it means the human response to God's
grace.[17] Often that response is an act of *imitatio Dei*.[18] So, Paul's *double
entendre* in Greek is an insightful exegesis of the correct sense of the
original Hebrew term in Scripture. Up until the coming of Christ, the
faithful response to the righteousness of God had been the attempt to
keep the commandments of the Torah. But with the full revelation of
the righteousness of God in the person of Christ, keeping these commandments as salvific is a rejection of the righteousness of God. It is a
claim to achieve salvation by the recipients themselves instead of being a response to the source of salvation itself. "When you have faith
in your heart that God has raised him [Christ] from the dead, you
shall be saved (*sōthēsthē*)" (10:9). Before Christ, the teleology of the
law had been positive; after Christ it is now (and forever) negative,
retroactively, that is.[19]

One final point must be made in concluding this brief representation of New Testament teaching about the relation of law and eschatology, and that is to better decide just what Paul means by "the law"
(*ho nomos*). Does it mean the whole Torah, all the commandments
given through Moses and the prophets? Or, does it mean only part of
the Torah? If the latter, then we must determine which commandments have been superseded by the coming of Christ and which remain intact. This has been a constant problem for Christian exegesis.
On the one hand, it has had to maintain some connection to Jewish
law in order to ward off the threat of Marcionism, for the logical conclusion of Marcionism's rejection of the Jewish people and Jewish revelation (and its law) was the rejection of the Lord God of Israel whom
Jesus called his Father. But Paul himself never severed his ties to either the Torah or to the Jewish people, and he would have certainly
been opposed to any Christian doing that.[20] On the other hand, Christian exegesis cannot interpret the New Testament in a way so Jewish

16. See, e.g., LXX on Gen. 18:19; Zech. 8:8.
17. See D. Novak, *The Election of Israel* (Cambridge: Cambridge University Press,
1992), pp. 125-38.
18. See B. Shabbat 133b re Exod. 15:2 (the opinion of Abba Saul).
19. For a most comprehensive treatment of Paul's complex relationship with the
law, see E. P. Sanders, *Paul and Palestinian Judaism* (Philadelphia: Fortress Press, 1977),
pp. 474-511.
20. See Romans 9-11.

that Christianity is seen as nothing more than an offbeat Jewish sect. Traditionally, this latter threat has been known as "Judaization."[21] So, in contrast to Marcionism, Christian exegesis of the New Testament, especially the Pauline epistles, has had to affirm some Jewish law as opposed to none; and in contrast to the Judaizers, it has had to affirm some Jewish law as opposed to most or all of Jewish law.

What emerges from the Pauline epistles, especially Romans, is that Paul affirms those aspects of Jewish law that are universal in scope. That means the prohibition of idolatry and all that it entails. And it means the virtually intact retention of Jewish moral law in its broad outlines. What distinguishes the Jewish law still to be kept from the Jewish law now taken as superseded is that the former is universal; the latter, by contrast, is what has been legislated based on the unique past experience of the Jewish people. Furthermore, what is universal in scope is that which is known to all humans even before any specific historical revelation. Thus Paul condemns the unrighteousness *(asebeia)* of the gentiles "because *(dioti)* that which is known of God is evident *(phaneron)* to them since *(gar)* God has made it evident to them, since what is invisible becomes evidently known *(nooumena)* from what has been created" (Rom. 1:18-19). In the next chapter, Paul speaks of the gentiles "who have not law but do by nature *(physei)* what the law contains . . . being a law unto themselves *(heautois eisi nomos)* . . . they bear witness through their conscience *(tēs syneidēseōs)* . . . the law written in their hearts" (2:14-15). It is clear why all Christian natural law proponents have referred to these words of Paul as their prime theological source.[22]

The difference between law retained and law superseded is that law retained pertains to present human nature, whereas law superseded pertains to past Jewish history. The coming of the kingdom of God, which Paul (and all Christians) see as being ushered in by the coming of Christ, introduces a posthistorical time into the world, which is the realm of eternity. The events of the life and death of Christ will be what are now celebrated because of this radical conclusion of all previous history. Nonetheless, it does not introduce a time when acts like murder, fornication, and deceit will now be permitted.

---

21. See Robert L. Wilken, *Chrysostom and the Jews* (Berkeley: University of California Press, 1983), pp. 66-94, 116-23.
22. See Thomas Aquinas, *Summa Theologiae*, 2/1, q. 91, a. 2.

That is because human nature still endures, and its redemption can hardly be seen as leading to a moral devolution. Redemption is meant to cleanse human nature of sin, not permit sins against human nature heretofore prohibited by the law, both Jewish and natural. Paul is anything but an antinomian. That is something the Reformers like Luther and Calvin were quick to emphasize when their Pauline-based revolt against the law of the Catholic Church was interpreted by some more radical than themselves to be a revolt against law per se in the name of God.[23]

3. The Question of the Repeal of the Commandments

In the century or so after the death of Jesus, especially after the destruction of the Second Temple in 70 C.E., Pharisaic Judaism, which is now better named Rabbinic Judaism, was in a process of profound reformulation and reevaluation. Both the loss of the central institution of Jewish national-religious life and the rise of a community that seemed to be deviating more and more from Judaism and the Jewish people called for a critical reexamination of much of the tradition. This was especially the case with eschatology, the issue over which the Christian community was beginning to declare its independence from Judaism. One sees this process of reexamination in the following rabbinic dispute from the second century of the Common Era:

> Ben Zoma expounded the verse "that you remember the day you went out from Egypt all the days of your life" (Deuteronomy 16:3): "the days of your life" refer to daytime; "all (kol) the days of your life" refer to nighttime. But the Sages say that "the days of your life" refer to this world; "all the days of your life" refer to the days of the Messiah. Ben Zoma said to them, is the exodus from Egypt to be remembered during the days of the Messiah? Is it not stated, "Behold days are coming, says the Lord, when it will no longer be said 'as the Lord lives who raised the children of Israel out of the land of Egypt,' but 'as the Lord lives who brought the stock of the House of Israel from the land of the North'" (Jeremiah 23:7)? They said to him that mention of the exodus from Egypt will not be extirpated from its place [in the

23. See Paul Althaus, *The Ethics of Luther*, trans. R. C. Schultz (Philadelphia: Fortress Press, 1972), pp. 25-42; John Calvin, *Institutes of the Christian Religion* 2.7.13-15.

liturgy], but the exodus from Egypt will be supplemental to mention of the [redemption from the rule of the foreign] kingdoms *(malkiyot)*. Mention of the foreign kingdoms will be primary *(iqqar)* and mention of the exodus from Egypt will be secondary *(tafel)*.[24]

There are two basic contexts of this dispute. Both concern mention of the exodus from Egypt, which plays a central role in all Jewish liturgy. Indeed, remembrance of the exodus from Egypt is the uniquely Jewish reason given in the Torah for many of the commandments one today would call "cultic" or "ritual." The first context is a discussion of whether or not mention of the exodus must be a regular part of evening worship. Ben Zoma opts for mention of the exodus being part of evening worship now in contrast to the coming-world when it will be redundant. The second context is in the Passover table service *(seder)*, the question being whether there will be a Passover celebration when the Messiah comes.[25]

Ben Zoma's total elimination of the obligation to mention the exodus from Egypt in the days of the Messiah is clearly the more radical option. However, it is also the one that seems closer to the post-exilic eschatology found in Scripture. There the messianic texts mention a radically changed world, one where the ties to past salvific events will be overcome. Thus Deutero-Isaiah speaks of "the new heaven and the new earth to stand before Me" (Isa. 66:22). Jeremiah speaks of the time when God will make a covenant "not like the covenant I made with your ancestors when I had to force them to be taken out from Egypt" (Jer. 31:31). Ezekiel speaks of the time when God "will open your graves and raise you up from your graves" (Ezek. 37:12). From all of these texts and more one sees that God's fulfillment of the covenant with Israel will so radically alter the world that the normal preconditions for the observance of the commandments of the Torah will be largely gone forever.

The earlier eschatological view is also seen in this rabbinic text. "Rabbi Abba bar Kahana said that God said 'a Torah will go forth from Me' (Isa. 51:4), namely, a new Torah *(hiddush torah)* will go forth from Me. Rabbi Berakhyah said in the name of Rabbi Isaac that God will *(atid)* be making a banquet *(ariston)* for His righteous servants in the

24. *Tosefta:* Berakhot 1.10.

25. See M. M. Kasher, *Israel Passover Haggadah* (New York: Shengold Publishers, 1964), pp. 54-57.

coming-future *(l'atid la-vo)*, where all who did not eat proscribed foods *(nevelot u-trefot)* in his world *('olam ha-zeh)* will be privileged *(zokeh)* to eat them in the coming-world."[26] From the standpoint of this strand of rabbinic theology, there would be no dispute with the New Testament about the "Son of Man is the lord of the Sabbath." These Rabbis would also agree that the law is overcome in the messianic future. And, obviously, the law to be overcome is the kind of law of which the Jewish dietary restrictions are the prime example. It is the law that has heretofore characterized the uniqueness of the Jewish people. Nevertheless, surely no one would have said that those who did not commit adultery in this world will have their pick of sexual partners in the next world, or that those who did not commit murder in this world will have their pick of victims in the next world.

It is quite clear from these and other similar texts that the coming-world will be based on a future experience so transforming that the very historical identity of the people of Israel will be radically altered, including all those rituals based on past, partially salvific, experiences. The House of Israel will remain because of God's everlasting covenant with her, but her characterizing acts will be fundamentally different. The new manifestation of this covenant in the coming-future will have the effect of attracting many gentiles to join the Jewish people, and that itself might explain why a new Torah will be needed for this radically transformed time.[27] But, surely, a promise that there will be no moral law in the end time could hardly be an attraction to the same God who gave the Ten Commandments.[28] So, these Rabbis would no doubt agree with Paul that the messianic time will elevate, not debase human nature, hence the basic law governing interhuman relations will remain intact, both for Jews and for gentiles.[29]

At this level, the debate, indeed the only essential debate, is

---

26. *Midrash Rabbah: Leviticus* 13.3.

27. See Isa. 2:1-4; 56:6-7.

28. For rabbinic recognition that the Christians (whom they called *minim*, "sectarians") regarded the Ten Commandments as the basic content of the Mosaic Torah to remain authoritative forever, see *Palestinian Talmud:* Berakhot 1.8/3c. For subsequent Christian emphasis of the unique normative status of the Ten Commandments, see Thomas Aquinas, *Summa Theologiae* 2/1, q. 100, aa. 3, 8; Calvin, *Institutes* 2.8.1.

29. The parallel to this in Rabbinic Judaism is that one who converts to the Jewish covenant (and who is "born again," cf. John 3:4-6) is in no way dispensed from moral obligations that Jewish law recognizes as binding on all humans. See B. Yevamot 22a; B. Sanhedrin 59a.

whether or not Jesus of Nazareth is the promised Messiah of the House of Israel. The Christians say yes; the Jews say no. That difference alone has been more than sufficient to keep Jews and Christians in two separate, indeed competing, communities since the first century. Nevertheless, this difference spawned some corollaries in the history of the Jewish-Christian relationship.

4. The Transformation of Jewish Eschatology

It seems almost inevitable, though, that with the increasing division between the Jewish community and the new Christian community, the difference over the messiahhood of Jesus of Nazareth would not only be a matter of *who* the Messiah is but it would also become a matter of *what* the Messiah is to do and *why* he is to do it. The original dispute was over whether Jesus of Nazareth was the Messiah or not. One can assume that the older Pharisaic position, for the most part, was that the commandments of the Torah will have already performed their propaedeutic function by the time the Messiah ushers in the kingdom of God. However, with the whole negative critique of the law by Paul, who asserted that the main function of the law is to show us how sinful we are rather than positively foreshadowing the kingdom of God, it seems that Jewish thought reasserted the value of the law in response. Any reassertion of a doctrine in the present is always more emphatic than the original assertion in the past.

If one can see the view of the Sages in contrast with that of Ben Zoma as at least a partial reaction against Christian eschatology, then one might reconstruct its logic as follows: We not only say that Jesus of Nazareth was not the Messiah because he did not remove Roman domination over us, but we also say that the very abrogation of the law made in his name also shows us that he was not the Messiah. We assert that the law will be in full force in the kingdom of God. In fact, we see the prime purpose of the kingdom of God to be to enable us to fully observe the commandments. Jesus' assertion that he came to fulfill the law for us instead of enforcing the law for us is a sure sign that he was not the Messiah. A true Messiah would have done the exact opposite. Thus, for example, the Rabbis had to admit that the Jewish revolutionary, Bar Kokhba (ca. 135 C.E.), was not the Messiah because he too failed to remove Roman domination over the Jewish people.

Nevertheless, he could have hardly declared the authority of the law to be now past and have, nonetheless, won the support of the leading Sage of his time, Rabbi Akibah ben Joseph, a man who died as a martyr for teaching the law in public.[30] Rabbi Akibah's belief that Bar Kokhba was the Messiah turned out to be a bad political judgment.[31] Yet it was not theologically unsound inasmuch as Bar Kokhba would have no doubt administered the full range of the commandments of the Torah had he been able to assume real messianic power. The most charitable view of Jesus of Nazareth, therefore, would be that he was one more would-be Messiah who failed. The true Messiah, then, would still have to be the object of hope, not memory.

The debate between Ben Zoma and the Sages is essentially over the question of whether or not "the commandments are to be nullified in the coming-future" (mitsvot betelot l'atid la-vo). The following rabbinic text reflects this debate in a new way:

> A garment in which there was detected threads of wool and linen (kla'yim) . . . one may make from it a shroud for a corpse. Rav Joseph said that this means that the commandments are nullified in the coming-future. . . . Rabbi Yohanan said that one may do so, and this follows Rabbi Yohanan's view concerning the verse "the dead are free" (ba-metim hofshi — Psalm 88:6), which means that a person is free from the commandments (hofshi min ha-mitsvot) when he dies.[32]

This text begins with the question of whether the scriptural commandment not to wear a garment in which wool and linen are mixed (shatnez — Deut. 22:11) applies to the shrouding of a corpse. Firmly believing in the resurrection of the dead, Rav Joseph infers that if this is permitted, and if corpses are to be resurrected in the clothing in which they were when buried, then the wearing of a forbidden garment could not be a problem at the time of the resurrection.[33] In other words, he gives a theological reason for a practical legal ruling. However, the earlier view of Rabbi Yohanan seems to come to the same practical conclusion, but for a different reason. He seems to avoid the theological question of the resurrection altogether and simply as-

---

30. See B. Berakhot 61a-b.
31. See Palestinian Talmud: Taaniyot 4.5/68d.
32. B. Niddah 61b.
33. See B. Berakhot 18a. Cf. Berakhot 17a re Exod. 24:11; also, Matt. 22:23-32.

sumes that the clothing of corpses is not the same as the clothing of the living.

Whereas Rav Joseph was a Babylonian Sage of the late third and early fourth centuries, Rabbi Yohanan bar Napaha was a Palestinian Sage of the third century. The difference in time and place is very important to bear in mind. Whereas Rav Joseph was a Sage in a time and place where very few Christians were found and where Christianity was not confronting Judaism in any direct way, Rabbi Yohanan (a contemporary of Origen and possibly someone who had disputed with him) was a Sage in a time and place (Tiberius) when Christianity was in major conflict with Judaism. This comes out in the following text on our question of the relation of law and eschatology: "Rabbi Yohanan said that although the Prophets and Hagiographa will be nullified in the [messianic] future, the five books of the [Written] Torah will not be nullified. What is his scriptural support? 'a great voice unending' (Deuteronomy 5:19)."[34] His colleague and brother-in-law, Rabbi Simon ben Laqish, went further and is reported in this same text to have included the Book of Esther and the oral traditions *(halakot)* in what will remain in force when the Messiah comes. It is doubtful whether Rav Joseph was even aware of the theological basis of Rabbi Yohanan's view since the above text from the Palestinian Talmud or anything like it is not even mentioned in the discussion of shrouds in the Babylonian Talmud.

The reason for the willingness to see no further need for the Prophets and Hagiographa is that their main function is taken to be the enunciation of messianic prophecy. As Rabbi Yohanan is also reported to have said, "all the prophets only prophesied about the days of the Messiah."[35] But, whereas the days of the Messiah will make prophecy's role passé, it will not have this effect on the commandments of the Torah. They are taken to be perpetually binding even — especially — when the Messiah will come. Because of his time and place, it is quite likely that anti-Christian polemic was an important part of Rabbi Yohanan's theological reflections.

---

34. *Palestinian Talmud:* Megillah 1.5/70d.
35. B. Berakhot 34b re Isa. 64:3.

5. Law and Faith

Rabbi Yohanan's further emphasis on the authority of the law, both in pre- and post-messianic time, is in full accord with the continual rabbinic emphasis on the sanctity of the Torah and the power of the commandments of the Torah to make the Jews who keep them the intimates of God here and now. Later on, in the face of the efforts of the much more politically powerful Christian community to proselytize the Jews in the Middle Ages, some Jewish scholars who were very familiar with Christian texts argued that there is no opposition between faith and the law but, rather, that the commandments themselves are faith-acts.[36] Therefore, anyone who denies the perpetual authority of the law is without true faith. One such scholar was Rabbi Moses ben Nahman of Gerona, subsequently known as Nahmanides, the leading Jewish jurist and theologian in Christian Spain in the thirteenth century. In fact, he was the leading Jewish spokesman in the most famous of the public disputations, commanded by royalty, that pitted Dominican theologians against Jewish theologians to prove — or try to prove — which faith is the true faith. This disputation took place in Barcelona in July of 1263.[37] Over and above the record of this disputation, it is clear from all his writing that Nahmanides knew Christian sources very well. This enabled him to defend Judaism in a most learned way, one showing great insight into the Christian basis for opposition to Judaism.

We see this great insight in Nahmanides' interpretation in his Torah Commentary (his central theological work) of the verse, "cursed is one who does not uphold the words of this Torah to do them" (Deut. 27:26). He writes:

> In my opinion this acceptance means that one acknowledges [the commandments] in his heart and that they are true in his eyes. . . . But if he denies any one of them or they are in his eyes nullified forever (betelah l'olam), he is surely cursed. Yet that is not so if he only transgresses one of them . . . for the verse did not say, "cursed is the

36. See E. E. Urbach, *The Sages*, vol. 1, trans. I. Abrahams (Jerusalem: Magnes Press, 1975), pp. 391-99.

37. See R. Chazan, *Barcelona and Beyond* (Berkeley: University of California Press, 1992), pp. 39-79.

one who does not do *(lo ya'aseh)* the words of this Torah; it says "who does not uphold *(lo yaqim)* the words of this Torah."[38]

There is little doubt that Nahmanides is arguing against Paul's interpretation of this verse (Gal. 3:10), for Paul uses it to show that everyone living under the law is cursed because no one can possibly observe all the commandments all of the time. Furthermore, Paul's interpretation uses the Septuagint's rendering of this verse as saying "all *(pasin)* the words of this Torah." The force of Paul's interpretation is that the observance of the law is all or nothing: either totally effecting salvation or totally preventing it, the latter being the curse of which the verse warns at the outset.

But Nahmanides turns Paul's interpretation on its head, so to speak. In his interpretation, faith is faith in the perpetual sanctity and authority in the Torah as a normative whole, even if one cannot possibly observe all of its commandments all of the time. It is not this faith but our human works that always lag behind it. Faith in God's law is itself salvific. For Nahmanides, then, it is not our works that remind us of our sin so much as our works attempt to put our faith in practice, knowing full well that faith in the God who gave the Torah is the same faith in the God who will finally redeem us forever.[39] And, moreover, this salvific faith is extended by Maimonides (d. 1205, and a great influence on Nahmanides' theology) to those gentiles who also accept the law that the Rabbis assumed is binding on them, even without full conversion to Judaism.[40] In the case of these gentiles, what is important is not their perfect observance of the law but rather their *acceptance* of the law as being from God and not from human invention. For some medieval Jewish authorities, this was the criterion for judging Christianity and Islam to be authentic kinds of monotheism and thus leading to the inference that true Christians and Muslims would indeed be worthy of being included with all Israel in the life of the coming-world.[41] In the case of Christianity, interestingly enough, this meant a Jewish validation of Christianity on Jewish, but

38. *Commentary on the Torah:* Deut. 27:26. See Novak, *The Theology of Nahmanides Systematically Presented,* p. 43.

39. See his *Commentary on the Torah:* Gen. 15:6.

40. *Mishneh Torah:* Kings 8.9-11 re *Tosefta:* Sanhedrin 13.2.

41. See D. Novak, *Jewish-Christian Dialogue* (New York: Oxford University Press, 1989), pp. 42-72.

certainly not Christian, terms. Whether or not Christians can possibly agree with this Jewish validation of them, at last minimally, is an important question for those Christians now engaged in the new and significant dialogue with Jews.

6. A Contemporary Review

There are two ways of formulating doctrinal theology: one *sub specie aeternitatis,* the other *sub specie durationis.* The former makes theological statements and insists they be regarded as dogmas, namely, propositions that have always been true and always will be. The latter addresses itself to a specific question arising at a point in the history of the faith-community, drawing upon the tradition's resources and coming to a tentative conclusion. Some doctrinal theologies have assumed that all theological statements must be presented as embodying perpetual truth. For them, all doctrine is dogma without history. Conversely, other doctrinal theologies have assumed that all theological statements can only be presented tentatively, that is, history without truth. They seem to fall into a type of historicism that reduces everything taught by the tradition to the relative meaning of those who have enunciated it, hence leaving it without any perpetual authority. Everything can be changed.

Rabbinic Judaism only assigned perpetual truth to propositions it could assume had the unanimous agreement of all the Sages that it was the teaching of the Sinaitic revelation. This meant that the majority of rabbinic teaching was, at least in principle, subject to subsequent repeal. For this reason, Jewish theology is well advised to draw as much as it can from critical-historical enquiry, so long as it does not adopt the historicist ontology some historians and philosophers have seen as being essential to this enterprise.

In the realm of law, the Rabbis spoke *sub specie aeternitatis* when they insisted that those commandments judged to be grounded in the Pentateuch (Written Torah) and those commandments judged to be undisputed ancient traditions going back to Sinaitic revelation (*halakot*) are not subject to any possible repeal by anyone in this world.[42] All of these traditions prescribe further details of scriptural

---

42. See B. Kiddushin 29a re Num. 15:23; B. Niddah 73a re Hab. 3:6.

commandments that cannot be derived through scriptural exegesis. The number of these scriptural commandments was finally determined to be six hundred thirteen, a determination that itself became very much a Jewish dogma.[43]

In the realm of theology, though, the number of dogmas was much smaller. In fact, one can say that here are really only three undisputed rabbinic dogmas: one, that the Torah is direct divine revelation *(torah min ha-shamayim)*; two, that the resurrection of the dead is revealed doctrine *(tehiyyat ha-metim min ha-torah)*; three, that God exercises authority in the world. One who denies the third dogma is deemed an "Epicurean" *(apiqoros)*, a follower of someone like the Hellenistic philosopher Epicurus, who could only admit to a totally absent god, which practically means no God at all.[44] The greatest Jewish dogmatist of all time, Joseph Albo, a fifteenth-century Spanish theologian (and the chief Jewish disputant at a famous disputation with Catholic theologians held in Tortosa in 1413-14), summarized these three dogmas more abstractly as being: one, God exists; two, God reveals his law; three, God judges how his law has been kept or violated in the world.[45] Whether or not one wants to limit the number of dogmas to these three (Maimonides posited thirteen), one could hardly argue that any of them had not been a dogma of Rabbinic Judaism.

From this dogmatic constellation, it seems that although the question of the relation of law and eschatology involves the two dogmas of the divinely given law and the final divine judgment of the dead, one cannot insist that the question of whether or not the law will be abrogated in the coming-future admits of dogmatic resolution. As such, it is best to identify a current theological dilemma for Jews and then select which view of law and eschatology seems to better address it than the other.

It has only been since the establishment of the State of Israel in 1948 that Jews have had the power Christians long had, namely, the political authority to enforce their religious law. In the State of Israel today, because of coalition politics, there are areas of Jewish law, especially regarding personal and marital status, that are enforced by the state. This has led to the political problem of the resentment of many

43. B. Makkot 23b-24a re Deut. 33:3.

44. M. Sanhedrin 10.1

45. *Sefer Ha'Ikkarim*, intro., trans. I. Husik (Philadelphia: Jewish Publication Society of America, 1929), 1:3.

secularist Jews and even non-Orthodox religious Jews against the Orthodox rabbinical establishment because of what they consider to be
undemocratic religious coercion. This resentment and the counter-
resentment of many Orthodox Jews against what they see as anti-
religious secularism lies at the heart of a major *Kulturkampf* facing
Israeli Jews and, by extension, all Jews throughout the world, since
the vast majority of all Jews everywhere have long been Zionists. But
the problem is more than just political in the usual secular sense. It is
theological.

The coercive policies of the rabbinical establishment are frequently justified by a messianic theology. This theology assumes that
the main function of the Messiah is to be the full enforcement of Jewish law as it pertains to both Jews and non-Jews living under Jewish
rule.[46] But if the enforcement of the law is the main function of the
Messiah, then it is inferred that one can also say that the further and
further enforcement of the law will actually bring the Messiah. Instead of enforcement of the law being a secondary function in a polity
of Jews who overwhelmingly want to live under the law, the enforcement of the law in this theologico-political vision is now the prime
task of a polity making the Messiah's rule possible, even probable.
Needless to say, this greatly enhances the political power of the
Rabbis and encourages the most authoritarian tendencies among
them. It is a prime recipe for the establishment of a *theocracy*, not in its
original sense of being in effect the kingdom of God *(theo-kratia)* but,
rather, a dictatorship of clerics.[47] Such a view, of course, virtually obscures the covenantal thrust of Jewish theology, namely, the view that
the relationship between God and Israel functions best when there is
a maximum of free persuasion and a minimum of coercion. As a famous rabbinic text teaches, even God could not force Israel to accept
his law.[48] Only when the Jewish people accepted it out of the freedom
of love did that law assume its true authority in the lives of the people.
There is certainly more to the covenant than democracy; nevertheless,
there is more of a democratic element in the covenantal reality than
contemporary Jewish theocrats can or will see.

46. See Maimonides, *Mishneh Torah:* Kings 11.1, 12.1-4.
47. For the original meaning of *theocracy,* see Josephus, *Contra Apionem* 2.164-67.
For a critique of contemporary Jewish theocrats, see D. Novak, *Covenantal Rights*
(Princeton, N.J.: Princeton University Press, 2000), pp. 25-32.
48. B. Shabbat 88a re Exod. 19:17. See Novak, *The Election of Israel,* pp. 163-77.

Because of the theologico-political dangers of religious coercion, it seems best for Jews today to see the end time as a totally apocalyptic event, one that will judge all our efforts in this world, not one that will simply extend the authority of the law with the concomitant human authority of interpreting and applying it in the world.[49] This might well be an excellent antidote to any historical triumphalism. Indeed, we Jews have learned the theologico-political dangers of historical triumphalism from the history of Christianity in its Constantinian manifestation. For Jews, the Constantinian notion of "Christendom" was the usual justification for our marginalization, even our persecution, by officially Christian societies. But, the notion of Christendom also led to great spiritual problems for Christians among themselves. This triumphalism led too many Christians to believe that the kingdom of God will only be realized when the power of the church is justified by political dominion, which always means *a* political regime. But the kingdom of God is not brought about, indeed it might well be impeded by, the mere extension of the power of the religious establishment through its official endorsement of one particular human regime on earth. Have we not seen from the history of Christianity that when the church officially endorses the state, it ends up by becoming an agency of the state? Isn't it better when the church is in the world but not of it?

Jews have much to learn about the bad political and spiritual consequences of certain forms of Christian eschatology. Christians have had much more experience with political power than we have had. The political consequences of any form of eschatology should be our prime criterion for selecting one form of eschatology rather than another at the point in history when that theological judgment has to be made, for what we think of the future is an essential factor in how we are to act here and now. And since the messianic element in Jewish theology is so profoundly political in its vision, its present implications cannot help but be profoundly political as well. We have much to learn about this from the political history of Christianity, something that should instruct Christians themselves even more.

The time when Jews rightly thought that they had to maximally distinguish themselves from Christianity is past. We have well survived Christian attempts to theologically incorporate us, and Christian

---

49. See Novak, *The Election of Israel*, pp. 252-55.

political hegemony over Jews is almost totally passé. We now have as much to learn from our similarities to Christians as we have to learn from our differences from them. The issue of the relation of law and eschatology is a prime case in point. Our more important task today in the world is how to handle our new power here and now. How do we offer it to glorify God's kingship and not use it to enhance our own importance? In the light of this task and the questions it raises, we are better advised, I think, to look to the end time as the apocalyptic conclusion of the time of the commandments and thus the initiation of a new time "no eye but God's has ever seen" — or even anticipated.[50] Can one think of any better prophylactic against the idealistic and ideological pretensions of all the great movements of modernity, be they secular or religious? At least *sub specie durationis,* theology, especially eschatological theology, might well function best *via negationis.*

---

50. See B. Berakhot 34b re Isa. 64:3. Cf. 1 Corinthians 2:9.

The Book of Revelation and Orthodox Eschatology: The Theodrama of Judgment

JOHN A. McGUCKIN

The Book of Revelation or the Apocalypse of John has exercised historically a dramatic effect on the churches of the West. It is a highly unusual book. It has often been called the only prophetic book in the New Testament canon. That, of course, largely begs the question what the word "prophetic" means. One of the most overused categories in late modern theology, it is one that intentionally elides historical phases in a way that often confuses issues more than clarifying them. One example of the difficulties involved in the notion of the Christian prophet understood historically (as opposed to the ubiquitous symbolic use of the word in contemporary theological discourse) can be demonstrated in the way that the early Christian structure of officers within the church, in the primitive ages, clearly included the itinerant prophet. That ancient liturgical text, the *Didache*,[1] advocates that the president who orders the great prayer of thanksgiving should give precedence to the prophets who come visiting, and allow them the presidency in sacred discourse. By the later third century the office of Christian prophet has entirely disappeared. And the result? As the office is abolished the role is symbolically "absorbed" into the other offices. This process of absorption moves forward in ways that are familiar to us in history. The enlargement of the role and office of

---

1. First to second century, from west Syria. See esp. chapters 11–13 of the same for instructions on the officers and the regulation of hospitality to itinerant prophets.

Episcopos and Presbyter, to the detriment of the other ancient parallel offices of Virgin, Widow, Prophet, *Koinonos,* and *Diakonos,* is a story well known. My point here is that the spiritual absorption of the concept of prophecy into the episcopal and presbyteral functions (of liturgical prayer and preaching) is synonymous with the actual historical abolition of the office from the hierarchical taxonomy of early Christianity. The title similarly disappeared from the acceptable range of christological acclamations at the end of the first century.[2] The rhetoric of appropriation may well mask the dynamic of suppression. A similar argument may be made with the Reformation-era revival of belief in the prophetic status of the people of God, a notion that similarly covered or articulated a massive realignment taking place in the theology and taxonomy of the authoritative offices recognized in the Christian church.

The Book of Revelation, insofar as it uniquely canonizes the office and function of the Christian prophet (and preserves one of the great utterances of one of that office's representatives), is an important and rare resource. The book, however, has not exercised anything like the influence over the churches of the East as it has in the West. This is surely an odd thing to consider. The very nature of the "prophetic idea" which it enshrines may provide the clue to this. For in this book the prophet giving sacred and ecstatic discourse also provides correction to the angels of the churches. This clearly means the presidents of the various local communities. The Semitic background of the Book of Revelation is quite obvious, even though it has come down to the churches in Greek, and it may be interesting to recall that the Syriac/Aramaic concept of angel is rendered semantically not as the "messenger" (*angelos* of the Greek tradition) but as the "watcher," and as such a more or less direct synonym of the Greek form that we have come to know far more familiarly as *episcopos* — overseeing president, or bishop. Prophets seem superior in this literature to *episcopoi,* but even so the prophet of the Apocalypse learns his message from angels, and is commissioned to announce it to the earthly angels who oversee the churches.

Why should the Book of Revelation have a lesser impact on the Eastern churches when, as is evident from its very language and geo-

2. See J. A. McGuckin, "Jesus' Self-Designation as a Prophet," *Scripture Bulletin* 19, no. 1 (Winter 1988): 2-11.

graphical setting, it rises from the heartland of the Eastern church in Asia Minor? It not only was resisted when it made its claim (rising from Western pressure) to enter the canon of Scripture but, more significantly perhaps, it has remained the one scriptural book that is never used in the vast body of texts that comprise the rich collection of Orthodox liturgical books.[3] This is not to say that eschatological thought is absent from the Eastern liturgies, far from it, but the Apocalypse is certainly not chosen to provide it.

The Book of Revelation focuses on the eschatological Lordship of the risen Christ who is now master of history. The central theme of the whole book is the notion of God's exercise of judgment over the world through his Christ. The martyrs demand redress at the heavenly throne (6:10; 16:7; 18:24) and the heavenly liturgy celebrates this redress given in the divine judgment (15:3-4; 19:1-2). The works of humankind are the criteria of their judgment.

The abundance of symbolic veiled signs is a feature of late prophetic-apocalyptic thought. Their presence is explicitly marked (1:20) and sometimes we are even given public explanations of their significance (5:6, 8; 13:18; 17:9-18). Most of the symbols fit with the general prior tradition of apocalyptic ciphers.[4] The understanding of

---

3. I can think only of a partial debt to Revelation 21:4, which speaks of the eschatological condition: "He will wipe away every tear from their eyes; there will be no more death and no more sadness. The world of the past has gone." This is reminisced in the liturgical prayers found in the office of intercession for the dead: "Shelter them in places of light, in places of green pasture, in places of refreshment, whence all pain, sorrow and sighing have fled away, and where the visitation of your Countenance rejoices all your saints from all ages." But the inspiration is a dim memory that has been substantially developed from a much wider conception of the glory of the eschaton, and set in a context of communion of love and vision more personally, if less dramatically, than the Book of Revelation manages.

4. I am indebted to the very useful summatic study of J. L. D'Aragon, "The Apocalypse," *Jerome Biblical Commentary*, ed. R. Brown, J. Fitzmyer, and R. E. Murphy (London, 1968), pp. 467-93. A woman is a people (12:1f.) or a city (17:1f.); horns denote power (5:6; 12:3), especially dynasties (13:1; 17:3f.); eyes connote knowledge (1:14; 2:18; 4:6; 5:6); wings signify angelic mobility (4:8; 12:14); a trumpet denotes the awesome heavenly communication of truth (1:10; 8:2f.); a sharp sword indicates the judgment of the Word (1:16; 2:12; 2:16; 19:15; 19:21); white robes indicate heavenly inhabitants of glory (6:11; 7:9, 13f.; 22:14); palms indicate martyrs' triumphs (7:9); crowns indicate exaltation to dominion (2:10; 3:11; 4:10; 6:2; 12:1; 14:14). The history of the use of the book in Christian hermeneutic from antiquity to the early twentieth century is set out in a fascinating article by A. Feuillet, "Les diverses methodes d'interprétation de l'Apocalypse et les commentaires récents," *L'Ami du Clergé* 17 (1961): 257-70.

prophecy is clearly ecstatic. The Spirit ravishes the seer (1:10; 4:2) and communicates to him through visions no less than 54 times in the book. There is constant angelic intervention (67 times) where the heavenly being explains and interprets what is happening to the earthly prophet.

The concept of apocalypse is mentioned only once in the whole book in the title verse (1:1). Elsewhere the author clearly prefers the concept of prophecy. He himself is a chosen prophet (22:9) and thus admitted to the company of the prophets to whom he often refers,[5] and whose writings have clearly governed his thought.[6] Like them, he is given a mission (10:11) and this mandate is communicated in his first vision (1:9-20). Hereafter he must write a book of prophecy (1:3; 19:10; 22:7; 10:18f.).

The work is set within a period of apocalyptic struggle between the empire and the church of God; between God and his saints on one side, and Satan and his agents ranged on the other. The martyrs have already entered into victory. The confessors, among whom we must surely place the author, also share in that anticipated victory and, as a corollary, exercise great power in the earthly church. We know this context from many other sources. It is the argument which even in the third century is troubling the church of Carthage when Cyprian is bishop, and can be seen reflected in the whole of the early Christian theologizing about martyrs and their status in the first three centuries.[7] The struggle of the confessor with the bishop as the decisive guide of the earthly community is one that will mark the Christian community profoundly across the centuries. The book represents a prophetic message that stands in continuity with the warnings of the ancient prophets. God is coming with an imminent judgment to overthrow the forces of evil. This central motif of God's just judgment is given as the speech of God in Revelation 21:6-8. The faithful will be

---

5. A concept that is found only twice in all other Jewish apocalypses, but appears in this book no less than seven times (10:7; 11:8; 16:6; 18:20; 18:24; 22:6; 22:9).

6. The book is dependent on Daniel, Ezekiel, Isaiah, Zechariah, the Psalms, and Exodus. There is no knowledge shown of later Jewish or proto-Christian apocalyptic literature. From the total of 404 verses, 278 contain an Old Testament allusion.

7. Cf. J. A. McGuckin, *Martyr Devotion in the Alexandrian School (Origen to Athanasius)*, Studies in Church History, vol. 30 (Martyrs & Martyrologies) (Oxford, 1993), pp. 35-45. Repr. in E. Ferguson, ed., *Recent Studies in Church History*, vol. 5 (Garland, Conn., 1999).

rewarded with exaltation; the lapsed Christians and the unbelievers will be punished for their apostasy. The publishing of this prophecy is meant to warn and inspire: to serve as a parenesis to a church in difficult times; to assert the church's unflagging belief that despite the manner in which history seems to be going against them, the Lord is the undisputed sovereign of all human times and his judgment will be vindicated.

The historical location is deliberately vague. Just as the Book of Daniel sets itself in a distant past while actually commenting upon the times of the later Maccabees as if they were the distant future, so the Apocalypse plays with the reader's sense of historical events. This is one of the reasons that we find the date of this work assigned to wildly varying times ranging from Claudius to Domitian.[8] The increased stress Domitian laid in his late reign (c. 90-96) on the application of the cult of the divine emperor[9] as a binding force for Asian society can explain much of the sense of anxiety in the book and its theological perspective that the persecution rises out of demonic resistance to God's reign.

The internal structure is organized from series of symbols and visions grouped by the "perfect" number seven. There are letters to the seven churches of Asia (2-3); the scroll sealed with seven seals (5:1–8:5); seven angels with seven trumpets (8:6–11:19); seven angels with seven bowls of God's wrath (15:1–16:21). As far as any overall coherent structure is concerned, no common agreement has been reached. Numerous theses involving editors and redactors of different times have been put forward. Scholars have argued a theory of compositions in sevens (comparable to the Johannine Gospel signs), or a mimicry of the compositional form of the OT prophetic books (which of course do not have a common structure anyway). The text itself is often chaotic and confusing. However, it does announce to the reader that it is organized on a double divine command: "Write down what you have seen; what is, and what is to come" (1:19). The recounting of the present events gives way to the warnings of the future woes and their glorious resolution in the liturgy of the kingdom. To this extent the structure is simple and twofold, although those divisions themselves

8. Revelation 17:9-11 suggests the reign of the sixth emperor Vespasian, but this is like taking the book of Daniel to belong to the period of Persian captivity.

9. He demanded the title: "Dominus et deus noster" (Suetonius, *Domitiani Vita* 13.4).

open up into complex subdivisions, based in turn upon discrete visionary epiphanies. The narrative of "what is," therefore, comprises the letters to the seven churches (2:1–3:22) and the narrative of "what is to be" is the series of seven visionary scenes. Prefacing and concluding this is an introduction and epilogue. The whole emerges in this form:

A. Introduction (1:1-20)
B. What Is: The Letters to the Seven Churches of Asia (2:1–3:22)
C. What Is to Come: The Eschatological Visions
   1. The Seven Seals (4:1–8:1)
   2. The Seven Trumpets (8:2–11:19)
   3. The Dragon and the Lamb (12:1–14:20)
   4. The Seven Bowls (15:1–16:21)
   5. The Fall of Babylon (17:1–19:10)
   6. The Final Advent of Christ the Judge (19:11–21:8)
   7. The Descent of the New Jerusalem: The Bride of the Lamb (21:9–22:5)
D. Epilogue (22:6-21)

One dominant motif of the whole book is the liturgical matrix that the author uses. In this he is typically "Asian" in his tradition. The heavenly liturgy as exemplified here is an ancient patristic extension of the Exodus typology. This is something that has survived strongly in all the paschal liturgies of the Eastern and Western churches.[10] The entrance of the church into the heavenly kingdom, the ultimate eschatological image, is conceived as the arrival of the elect people on the far side of the river, the New Paradise of the Promised Land. The sacrifice of the Pascha Lamb and the Exodus from evil are the preludes to the New Age. This structure of typological thought underpins most of the ancient church's liturgical-eschatological theology. In the case of the Book of Revelation[11] the Exodus typology clearly serves as an organizing *idée maitresse*. The people of God are characterized as Israel. The Twelve Tribes represent the whole church

10. For an interesting discussion see M. H. Shepherd, *The Paschal Liturgy and the Apocalypse* (London, 1960).

11. See, for example, J. Daniélou, *From Shadows to Reality: Studies in the Biblical Typology of the Fathers* (London, 1960), pp. 153-226.

(7:4-8). The whole story of liberation is culminated in the sacrifice of the Lamb (5:12), and the great liberation is compared to crossing the sea of glass to escape the Beast and then singing the canticle of Moses as a victory hymn (15:2). The revelation is heralded with all the signs given at Sinai: trumpets (8:7), thunder, and lightning (8:5); and the punishments given to the world recall the plagues of Egypt: hail (8:7), the turning of the waters into blood (8:8; 16:3); the turning of day into darkness (8:12; 16:10); and the plague of locusts (9:3). Similarly, there is a sustained theme running throughout, of the New Para-dise.[12] Within this typology we notice how Christ's triumph over the serpent reverses and heals[13] the defeat of Genesis.[14] We see also how the church is the New Eve adorned as Bride[15] in a New Paradise where all pain and suffering and tears are wiped away.[16] The New Jerusalem is itself described in paradisal terms with a river of life running through it, and a health-giving tree[17] growing there.

All of this mounts up to an extended paschal typology. It is, in highly apocalypticized format, the selfsame eschatology that we find continued in the universal tradition of the church in the later patristic authors, that the kingdom of God is the paschal victory of the Christ, which ushers in a new paradisal age for the elect people of God. I shall come back to this later, but I would like to emphasize now an impor-tant aspect of this doctrine. The separation of soteriology and ecclesi-ology from eschatology is absolutely impossible. Far from ecclesiology being a later elaboration and even a diminution of the eschatological sensibility of the early church, it is abundantly clear (even in the most apocalyptic of all Christian books) that ecclesiology is the very fundament of what we mean by eschatological hope. To speak of one is to describe the other.

---

12. It is to culminate, as we shall see, in the millenarist idea that this paradise will descend from heaven to earth — an idea the universal church decisively rejected in its conflict with the later Montanist version of the idea, and ultimately came to regard as unworthy of representing the notion of the paradisal hope of the eschaton.

13. This is perhaps the (liturgical-typological) origin of the Asia Minor soteriological theology of the *Apokatastasis*, as evidenced in Irenaeus, which was to run on to develop from an Asian *theologoumenon* into a veritable aspect of the universal Christian tradition.

14. Cf. Rev. 20:2.

15. Cf. Rev. 21:2.

16. Cf. Rev. 21:4.

17. Cf. Rev. 22:1-2; Rev. 22:14, 19; Ezek. 47:1, 12.

The selfsame concern can be seen in that other intriguing survival from the hand of an early Christian prophet in the primitive church — the Shepherd of Hermas. This book too was, in the fourth century, regarded by many churches as canonical scripture; and was even bound up as the last of the New Testament books in that great Pandect manuscript that was possibly commissioned from Caesarea by Constantine for his new churches at Tyre and Jerusalem — the Codex Sinaiticus. Like Revelation, it was subsequently sidelined; indeed, removed deliberately from the canon, albeit for odd reasons — the protests of the Western theologians, led by Tertullian, that it was too liberal in its doctrine of forgiveness.

In the famous vision of the Tower that was in process of being constructed, the prophet again asks the angel the meaning of his vision. The context gives us to understand clearly enough that the Tower is the church in progress of being built. When Hermas asks the angel:

"In regard to the Ages, is there now to be a summation?"

he receives, albeit apocalyptically from the angel, the rather flattened apocalyptic response:

"Foolish man! Do you not see that the Tower is in course of being built? When the Tower is finished and constructed then shall come the End. And I tell you it will not be long. But ask me no more questions. Let you and all the saints be content . . . with the manner in which I renew your spirits."[18]

Hermas, following the Pauline doctrine that the End has been extended to allow the church time for repentance and the world time for evangelization, repeats the teaching that the ecclesial mystery, the working-out of God's plan of salvation, is itself the mystery of the eschaton, and not other to it.

The Book of Revelation clearly emanates from the churches of Asia Minor. And it is the patristic writers of this tradition who are the first to claim it as apostolic literature. In contrast to the Alogoi movement, which rejected both the Fourth Gospel and the Apocalypse as works of the docetic heretic, the Asian teacher Cerinthus, the Asia Minor theo-

18. Shepherd of Hermas, *Vision* 3.8.9.

logians claimed both books for the apostle John, and thereby laid the basis of their claim for its place in the canon. In the first half of the second century the anonymous author of the John Apocryphon sees Revelation as the work of the apostle,[19] as does the second-century Asian theologian Melito of Sardis.[20] The same approach is found in Papias of Hierapolis,[21] the early commentator on the Sayings of Jesus, and (like the author of Revelation) another chiliast from Asia Minor. The Samaritan philosopher Justin Martyr[22] (who in some circles is credited as having translated the work into Greek for a Roman audience) also believes in its apostolic authorship. His fellow countryman Irenaeus also gives witness to the same tradition of reverence.[23] All of these writers can be collectively grouped as oriental theologians of one form or another who witness to the Asia-Minor millenarist tradition, a tradition given the only voice that was not destined for suppression by the post-Constantinian Eastern church, in Revelation 20:1-6. The last two of this series, Irenaeus and Justin, also demonstrate for us how, at an early period, the Asian tradition had moved to major Western centers of commerce; notably Lyons, Rome, and North Africa. It was to be in these occidental ecclesiastical centers that the Asian apocalyptic tradition would survive longer than in Asia Minor, and last long enough (moderated in patristic times through the relative absorption of Montanist principles in the Latin West, compared to their relative suppression in the East) to enter the greater Christian tradition in its Western form, through Tertullian, Victorinus, and Lactantius.

The tradition of the apostolic authorship of the book is witnessed also in the early Alexandrian writers, who have no connection with Asia Minor, such as Clement[24] and Origenes,[25] but it is very quickly

19. Cf. A. Hembold, *NTS* 8 (1961-62): 77-79.

20. He is first described in a letter of Polycrates to Pope Victor in the time of the Quartodecimans controversy as a "continent living wholly in the Spirit" (Euseb., *HE* 5.24.2-8), though Eusebius perhaps confuses the issue by later calling him the Episcopos of the Church of Sardis (*HE* 4.13.8; 26.1). The recovery in 1960 of his Peri Pascha from the Bodmer papyrus renewed interest in him as an important early Asian theologian. We find in him a typically Asian concern with paschal eschatological symbolism.

21. According to the later commentator Andrew of Caesarea.

22. *Dialogue with Trypho* 81.4.

23. *Adv. Haer.* 4.30.4; 5.26.1.

24. *Paed.* 2.119.1; *Quis Dives Salvetur* 42.

25. *Comm. Jn.* 2.5, 45.

rejected by the later commentators beginning with Dionysius of Alexandria who, on the basis of his independent study, concluded that the language, style, and thought of the Gospel and First Letter of John show that Revelation must be from another hand. Dionysius identified this author with "John the Presbyter" of Ephesus.[26] After that point the book was at the center of a storm of opposition to its canonicity in the East. Most of the bishops of the Asian church in the later third century rejected it. In the aftermath of the Montanist movement, they found too many of the problematic "New Prophecy" tenets represented in the text: the nature of Christian prophetic inspiration as ecstatic; the superior authority of the prophet to the bishop; the descent of paradise to earth; the millenarist reign; and the strong advocacy of eagerness for martyrdom.[27] Each one of these points was to be strongly opposed in the traditions of the other Eastern churches, and not least in the original heartland, in Asia Minor itself, when the local *episcopoi* gathered synodically to resist the Montanist movement.[28] We might particularly note that one chief point of objection (and it is perhaps the reason why the whole office of prophet fell into disuse) was the apocalyptic manner of subordinating rational reflection to visual imagination — to visions as media of authoritative discourse. In the Christian theological literature of the third to fourth centuries and onwards, the turning away from the medium of epiphany and waking vision is very noticeable, and increasingly marks off the Christians from the religiosity of their contemporaries.[29] It is often presumed, perhaps because the bureau-

26. Eusebius, *HE* 3.39; 7.25, 16.

27. One of the chief reasons Montanism had been regarded with distaste was the manner in which the Christian faithful were called upon to volunteer themselves for martyrdom. When this was done it put the whole body of the faithful in a local region at risk, and so enthusiastic zealotry in time of persecution was denounced by synods of Christian leaders from the late second century onwards. When Montanism was exported to Rome and North Africa it brought many of the same items of agenda with it, as can be seen from the late writings of Tertullian and clearly in the crisis that Cyprian experiences with his confessors.

28. It has often been maintained in recent studies of the Montanist crisis that doctrine was not at issue — merely a struggle over church order and offices. I think such a view cannot be sustained.

29. See, for example, the remarkable story recounted in the *Alphabetical Collection of the Sayings of the Desert Fathers*, trans. B. Ward (London, 1981), p. 160, under the title of Abba Olympius, where the Egyptian priest wonders how the Christian monks are so deprived of epiphanies.

cratic approach springs more readily to the modern mind (even though the issue of the organization of the churches at this period is still a largely unknown factor), that the point of dispute in the Montanist crisis was one of authority model. The fact that the Christian communities in general decisively turn away from the state of waking vision, or the prophetic trance, as an acceptable medium for receiving divine epiphany ought to be observed more than it has been. It will not be until the high Middle Ages that either the Eastern or the Western churches will turn again to the vehicle of mystical vision, and then too with indecisive results.

All of the great biblical commentators of the Syrian school reject the Book of Revelation as canonical, witnessing to the universal tradition of the churches of Syria that stands against this text. The canonical lists of the Greek church continued to omit the Revelation fairly frequently, and many biblical manuscripts up to the ninth century routinely excluded it from the canon of New Testament books. It was undoubtedly the authority of Athanasius who advocated it should be accepted, so as to bring the canon lists of the Eastern and Western churches into harmony, that accounted for its eventual inclusion in the Eastern canon. Even so, in practice that canonicity was massively qualified. The almost complete deletion of this text from any major Greek liturgical formation — despite the obvious and illuminating liturgical matrix of the original writing — is a study in how the ancient tradition of the church often defined itself in paradoxes and decisions that were subject to massive historical qualifications. Even as it canonically accepted the Book of Revelation as a sacred text, the Eastern tradition ensured that its influence would be minimalized in the praxis of its abandonment in the liturgical troparia.

Iconographically, the Book of Revelation has exercised more of an influence. The icons of Michael as war angel lean heavily on Revelation 8:2–10:7, but this is an iconic type that is not noticeable in the early or classic periods of icon-writing in the Orthodox tradition, and seems rather to be an early modern phenomenon. The portrayal of Christ enthroned on a rainbow and seated on a throne surrounded by the four living creatures is something that is far more common, and certainly owes allegiance to the iconic symbols of the Book of Revelation. But here again, the reliance on the concept of judgment as maintained in the biblical text is radically qualified by the iconic tradition of the depiction of the Christ in Judgment. Orthodox tradition develops new themes and insights into the eschatological judgment that surface from a far wider understanding of the Christian tradition. What I have in mind most particularly is the set of overlapping and sometimes contrasting symbols that iconic theology can publish simultaneously without worrying about the strict logical coherence that is more dominant and necessary in a preached discourse or a written text. In the case of the iconic tradition of Christ enthroned in judgment, the common theme of Orthodox iconography is to depict Christ enthroned as priest-emperor on the throne of the apocalypse. It is a severe scene. Christ, in accordance with the awesome and hieratic nature of the text of Revelation, sits in judgment over a sinful world. And yet, the tradition goes further than the single book. The severe Christ is never shown with the same severity as is often the case in icons of the Pantocrator in church domes. Christ enthroned in judgment frequently has an aspect of sublime peace and mercifulness. The Gospel book is held open on his left knee (the side of the reprobate) while his right knee, the side of the elect, is traditionally the place the believer comes to venerate the icon, kissing the knee of Christ in obeisance. As believers approach the icon, like the soul anticipating its final judgment, they realize their failure to observe the gospel charter of their judgment, but at that same moment are able to read the text of the Gospel as it lies open on the knee of Christ. Here in all its mystery is the supreme text of the Last Judgment of the Soul: a text which the church has carefully selected to represent its insight into the Apocalyptic Judgment. And what is the normal text we find here? It is not something from the Book of Revelation but from the Lord's discourses in Matthew's Gospel:

> "Come to me all you who labour and are heavy burdened and I will give rest to your souls."[30]

What an extraordinary theological genius is represented here iconically! The severity of the throne of judgment and the hieratic posture of Christ are all tempered by the right hand held in blessing and this profoundly comforting text laid open to the worshiper. The ultimate theology is that the Judgment's quintessentially awesome character is most profoundly known in the mystery of God's compassion.

---

30. Matt. 11:28.

The mercy of God is itself awesome. Experiencing this abyss of mercy sears the soul — so it is for the living person who studies the living gospel of Christ, and so, the church teaches in its iconography, will it be for the dead in their judgment. The mercy of God will sear and wound, but also purify, the selfish hearts of creatures. Eschatology is thus the hope of our healing, and our reconciliation into communion.

The iconic themes of the Book of Revelation had a much different history in the West. The figure of Christ enthroned above the seven lambs is common in Western art. In the high Middle Ages and on into the baroque the concepts of the Four Horsemen (Rev. 6:1-17), the Lamb on top of Mount Zion from which flows the four rivers of Paradise, the Fall of Babylon, the Seven Seals being opened, and the New Jerusalem, are all popular and dominant motifs in manuscript illumination, tapestries, and wall paintings. The church frescoes of the Last Judgment also take their dominant motifs of the mouths of Hell from the tone established by the book. Iconic frescoes, such as the famous scene of the Judgment at the Final Resurrection at Voronets in Romania, also show similar ideas in Orthodox iconography. Here, however, it has to be remarked that these are late and Westernized influences, but unlike the Western examples, such frescoes of the Judgment are on the outside of the west wall of the Voronets church. The icon of Christ enthroned as merciful Judge is a more mystical doctrine for the initiate. The image of the Mouth of Hell belching fire is an image reserved for those who are not yet initiated and therefore not yet allowed to enter the church building proper. Once again, therefore, we see an unspoken struggle taking place in Eastern Christian tradition, keeping the influence of the Book of Revelation in check. One smaller example of the same thing can be seen in the remarkable 82nd canon from the Quinisext Council in Trullo[31] of 691, which actually forbade under terms of severe ecclesiastical penalty the depiction of Christ as Lamb in any church of the Christian Orient. This is in marked contrast to Western religious theology and art, where this image remained one of the staple christological symbols of the Latin world, even through the Reformation and into the modern period. In early theological thought we can see the Lamb-typology being advocated by

---

31. That is, in the imperial balcony of the Great Church at Constantinople. It was concerned with regularizing the ancient canons, and in turn was confirmed by the 7th Oecumenical council at Nicaea in 787. Cf. *Pedalion*, trans. D. Cummings (1957; repr. New York, 1983), pp. 386-87.

the millenarist theologian Justin Martyr[32] and the Asia Minor theologian Melito of Sardis[33] before it becomes a standard Christology of the patristic West.[34] There are no fewer than 28 references to the symbol of Lamb in the Book of Revelation, and though the issue of John the Baptist pointing to the Christ and calling him the "Lamb of God" was an important eucharistic *theologoumenon* for the patristic Greek world,[35] to have abolished it as a forbidden symbol speaks volumes. The canon gives it to understand that the Lamb as a depiction of Christ belongs to the "old world" of typological shadows and lies under the aegis of John the Forerunner, the last of the prophets of the old covenant. It is abundantly clear that the compilers of this canon have no conception of the use of the Lamb as a christological symbol in the scheme of the Book of Revelation. It simply does not figure in their view of the gospel tradition. The depiction of the evangelists as eagle, lion, ox, and man is also condemned as "unworthy." Their apocalyptic beast-ciphers are allowed in addition to the human icon of the evangelists, but never in substitution for them. In this the Eastern iconic tradition also marks a divergence with that found in the West.

If we were to consider what the Byzantine liturgical tradition, which is highly eschatological in its tone and content, instinctively turns to for its apocalyptic imagery, the answer seems to be the image of the returning bridegroom as presented in Luke's parable of the wise and foolish virgins. Already between the time of Jesus' delivering of this parable of the kingdom (which fits in with his general custom of depicting the character of the impending rule of God in terms of the celebrations of harvest or marriage feast),[36] and the interpretation of

32. *Dialogue with Trypho* 40.1.

33. *Peri Pascha* 5.67.71.

34. Tertullian, *Adv. Iud.* 10, 18; Cyprian, *Ep.* 63; Lactantius, *Div. Inst.* 4.26.36-39; Gaudentius, *Tract.* 3.21 & *Tract.* 6.11; Gregory, *Illiberitanus Tract.* 9.

35. Cf. Ps. Hippolytus, *In Sanctum Pascha* 32; Clement of Alexandria, *Paed.* 1.51; Origen, *Peri Pascha.* para. 9. SC 36. ed. Nautin, p. 84. fn. 1; also *Hom.* 13 in Lucam; also *In Joannem* 6.51, 52; Epiphanios of Salamis, *Haer.* 69; Cyril of Jerusalem, *Cat.* 19.3; Theodore of Mopsuestia, *Com. in Joannem* 1.29; Isidore of Pelusium, *Ep.* 4.162; Cyril of Alexandria, *Com. in Joannem* 7; Gelasios of Cyzicos, *Hist. Eccl.* 2.31. 6.

36. There are numerous examples of Jesus' comparison of God's impending judgment as an act of reconciliation such as witnessed in villages that celebrate the festivals. Common to all the ideas is the image of abundance as a sign of God's blessing in forgiveness, and the act of mutual communion (common eating), which also underlies that supreme prophetic sign Jesus chooses to encapsulate his mission — the sign of Eu-

it by the evangelist's community, we see the movement to a more overtly eschatological interpretation of the marriage feast as a judgment on those whose inattentiveness to the news of reconciliation makes them unfit to enter into the experience of the joy. In the final version of the parable as presented in Luke the attention has already moved from the kingdom's character to the issue of the disciple's preparation for it, something that is clearly seen also in Luke 12:35-48, the discourses on being ready for the master's return. This is a puzzle that particularly obsesses the Lukan eschatology, which throughout wonders if the Second Advent will be open and dramatic or secretive and spiritually internal.[37] The Eastern Christian liturgical tradition, however, has ironed out the hermeneutical problem. Here it is clear that the Lord will return as a bridegroom. The soul must prepare itself assiduously through repentance and constant awareness that its unworthiness precludes it from the joy of the kingdom, but with the constant presupposition that the mercy of the returning bridegroom will have a marked bias — not to exclude those who are worthy of exclusion: a paradox of salvation explained by the perennial belief in the mercy of God whose power to save is never exhausted, "since all things (even the salvation of the lost) are possible to God."[38] In its daily midnight office the Eastern liturgy summarizes this eschatological expectation in its prayer:

> Behold the bridegroom cometh in the middle of the night. Blessed is that servant he shall find awake. Unworthy is that servant he shall find heedless. Beware then my soul lest you be borne down by sleep, lest you be given up to death and be shut out from the Kingdom. Instead rouse yourself and cry out: Holy are you our God! Through the prayers of the bodiless powers have mercy on us.[39]

And again in the same service:

> Rouse yourself my soul and bring to mind that most fearful day. Be vigilant and enkindle your dark lamp and make it radiant with oil; for

---

charist. Cf. J. McGuckin, "The Sign of the Prophet: The Significance of Meals in the Doctrine of Jesus," *Scripture Bulletin* 16, no. 2 (Summer 1986): 35-40.

37. Compare Luke 17:20-21, and the separate juxtaposed pericope of Luke 17:23-25.

38. Cf. Luke 18:26-27.

39. The Midnight Office for weekdays.

you do not know when you will suddenly hear that voice which shall cry out: Behold the Bridegroom comes to you! Mark then, my soul, that you do not sleep like those five foolish virgins left outside and vainly knocking upon the door. Rather endure in all vigilance that you might meet Christ our God with rich oil, and that he might grant you the fair bridal chamber of his Glory for evermore.

Brian Daley's recent book on patristic eschatology[40] tells us a quite extraordinary fact (which is almost true) that it is the first full monograph ever to be devoted to the subject. His excellent bibliography[41] in that study collates all the seminal work that had gone on before him in the form of smaller and more focused pieces of research or longer German monographs with which he takes issue.[42] He finds a trend in early Christian eschatology that moves from the imminent expectation of an apocalyptic end to a more future-oriented view that works towards a more coherent doctrine of creation, a developed theology of the ongoing rule of the risen Lord, and an elaboration of a more person-centered belief in the doctrine of the resurrection of the believer that extends into a fuller Christian anthropology. Some commentators suggest that such a shift also relates to the socio-economic condition of the church in any given period. Social problems, it would appear, produce a more lively eschatological awareness than periods of prosperity and calm. This sounds plausible enough. If only it fitted the real history the picture would be ideal. But it doesn't. It only partially correlates with real events and so cannot be taken as a macro-explanation. The Christians in the third and fourth centuries lived in no less troubled times than those of the first and second. The third century saw one of the greatest inflation problems ever to have occurred in the history of the empire. Even the so-called establishment of the church in the Pax Constantiniana is really a retrospective euphemism, because the bloody civil wars and the collapsing of borders that mark

40. B. E. Daley, *The Hope of the Early Church: A Handbook of Patristic Eschatology* (Cambridge, 1991).

41. Daley, *The Hope of the Early Church*, pp. 266-87.

42. Among those works we might single out for particular attention the contributions of Georges Florovsky, "The Patristic Age and Eschatology: An Introduction," in *Aspects of Church History*, Collected Works, vol. 4 (Nordland, Mass., 1975), pp. 66-67. Also: G. W. H. Lampe, "Early Patristic Eschatology," *Scottish Journal of Theology*, Occasional Papers 2 (London, 1953): 17-35; and A. J. Visser, "A Bird's Eye view of Ancient Christian Eschatology," *Numen* 14 (1967): 4-22.

the era of Constantine to Theodosius represent the empire in its most perilous condition. Yet it is these very centuries that see the move away from the apocalyptic mindset.

What we witness in the study of the Book of Apocalypse, and its reception in the East, is something that should make us be more wary of taking this linear view of the development of Christian eschatology as dominantly as many have suggested. The conception of the linear drive of history to a teleotic summation is, of course, the quintessential philosophical contribution of the apocalyptic movement, but it is, at one and the same time, logical nonsense. Once one takes the symbolic image of summation of history as a factive chronological indicator of the Next Age, one makes the dreadful mistake of believing that the very thing which lies outside time can be depicted as the last act of a time-bound sequence. Put this another way: the church's belief in the advent of Jesus, his Resurrection that saves the race, and his Second Coming, is a belief in the redemptive significance of his action for the totality of world history. Such acts are eschatological precisely because they transcend history, and by transcending it give its ultimate meaning. They summate the destiny of the world not as an event within the sequence of world history, but as the *telos* that includes it and far from merely ending it, rectifies, redeems, and heals it.

Behind this idea of a linear move in Christian theology, it is argued, is the way in which primitive expressions of communal hope tend to be modified into conceptions of the individual's salvation — a move, if you like, from communitarian eschatological conceptions to notions of the individual's afterlife and judgment. But it would be wrong to elevate this to the status of a guiding structural development. Such a notion of linear development has been fostered particularly by the nineteenth-century rediscovery of the category of apocalyptic. The conception of the systematic rereading of Jesus' message as out-and-out apocalyptic, heavily emphasized in Schweitzer's *Quest of the Historical Jesus* (the so-called First Quest), has, however, been very much qualified by the findings of the New and Third Quests. It is abundantly evident that the strict categorization of Jesus of Nazareth as an out-and-out apocalypticist fails to do service to the abundance of material even in the earliest Jesus Logia which does not fit into this category. To excise everything that does not equate with apocalyptic from the earliest Jesus tradition and allocate it to the earliest level of apostolic manipulation of the kerygma is, to say the least, a questionable use of the evidence. It is

surely time to take radical stock once more. The divergent findings of
the Third Quest have, if nothing else, shown how much of the Jesus material can be contextualized in his own day and milieu without obses-
sive reliance on the genre of apocalyptic-prophetic. Even if we were to
admit that the apostolic generation diverted the ecclesial tradition away
from imminent apocalyptic thought to a more personalized sense of individual communion with the risen Christ, the fact that this happened
even before the composition of the Gospel narratives undermines the
presupposition that such a development is patristic as opposed, for example, to biblical or apostolic in conception. The fact is that the scheme
of applying linear models of development of theology to explain the
early church's complex and multifaceted beliefs in eschatology (of
which apocalyptic was one aspect) is a hangover from German liberal
Protestant scholarship of the late nineteenth and early twentieth centuries. It served an important purpose. Now it must be finessed, and perhaps even laid aside as a useful schema, at least as a model of collective
understanding of the early Christian eschatology.

If we are clear on the distinction that must be drawn between the
concepts of apocalyptic and eschatological, with the former being
merely one mode among others of the latter, then perhaps we may be
led to consider the possibility that apocalyptic was a mode of discourse that rapidly ran out of favor in the early Christian community
precisely because it was not sufficiently deep in its eschatological understanding, and had attempted to give voice to that which could not
be properly voiced. The device, employed in the Book of Revelation, of
having angels speak to the prophet those things the earthly prophet
could not comprehend still does not save him from the charge of having handled the eschatological imperative in a far less refined manner
than the apostle Paul, who deliberately lapses into silence as the best
indicator of his visions of the heavenly liturgy in 2 Corinthians 12:1-6.
It is with a similar discretion that the apostle advocates the careful
regulation of the prophets in the early communities, so that they do
not become disordered in their enthusiasm. The prophet here (and we
may note the antiquity of the dating) is subject to the mandate of the
apostle,[43] and the spirit of prophecy the prophet receives is never to
be presumed to be ecstatic or irrational.[44] Paul, therefore, made no ac-

43. 1 Cor. 14:36-40.
44. 1 Cor. 14:32.

cidental connection in his letters to the Corinthians between the eschatological and the ecclesiological, just as Jesus himself presumed that every discourse on the kingdom presupposed the context of the Elect People of God and the destiny of salvation the Lord of Israel had prepared for them.

If we turn to Origen, who retains this deep emphasis on ecclesiology as the core of the eschatological insight, and has often been caricatured as the supreme example of the patristic tendency to "flatten out" the apocalyptic dimension of the primitive church in the cause of an extended ecclesiology and a highly individualist understanding of the immortal soul, then we can see that far from abandoning the tradition of the gospel's eschatology, he is rather being faithful to the New Testament tradition when he summarizes the issue succinctly as a matter of love in the communion of the saints. In his Commentary on Romans he describes the eschatological mystery in these corporately ecclesial terms:

> The Apostle thus expresses his hope that the whole body of the Church shall be restored. Nor does he think that the perfect things can be given over to individual members until the universal body shall be gathered together as one.[45]

It is a text that Georges Florovsky "translates"[46] as follows:

> History goes on because the Body has not yet been completed. The "fullness of the Body" implies and presupposes a re-integration of history, including the Old Dispensation, i.e. "the end." Or, in the phrase of St. John Chrysostom, "then is the Head filled up, then is the Body rendered perfect, when we are all together, all knit together and united."[47]

We see a similar understanding in Gregory Nazianzen, who describes the final eschatological state as a progress to the third age[48] under the emerging visibility of the Holy Spirit of God, the Spirit who had not formerly been clearly disclosed.[49] The first two ages were di-

---

45. Origenes, *Com. in Rom.* 7:5.
46. G. Florovsky, "The Patristic Age and Eschatology: An Introduction," in *Aspects of Church History*, pp. 66-67.
47. John Chrysostom, *In Ephes. Hom.* 3.1.23.
48. Fifth Theological Oration (*Orat.* 31.25).
49. Cf. John 7:39.

vine transitions for the human race (metástaseis) and were accompanied by seismic shakings[50] of the cosmic order. The third transition will be an equally great shaking of the world order, completing and superseding the Old and New Testaments themselves. It begins in the church's identification and recognition of the divinity of the Holy Spirit, is proven by its trinitarian confession, and then demonstrated in the Christian's ability to manifest the fruits of the Spirit, not least in the perspicacity of his or her theological judgment, as the Holy Spirit "teaches us all things."[51]

According to Gregory:

> This third seismic shaking is the change from the present state of things to what lies unmoved and unshaken[52] beyond.[53]

He elaborates this whole pneumatic-eschatological argument in the context of advising his antagonists to be very wary of insisting on the principle of *Sola Scriptura*. For Gregory the very interpretation of the authentic mind of the Scripture is a product of the mystical initiation which the Holy Spirit confers on the believer, in the church. To use the Scripture to deny the deity of the Spirit (as the Eunomians did) is, for him, the quintessential mark of a whole system of theology that has gone astray at the very root of its principles and ordering.

This is the very heart of what Florovsky used to call "the mind of the Fathers," and it perhaps also demonstrates how the recognition of the true tradition of the church in each generation is never merely a mechanical act of accumulating all that has gone before it chronologically, or merely repeating as proof-texts central traditional formulations. The discernment of the shape and movement of the Tradition, within the manifold traditions of theology and culture, is something other to this, and calls for an exercise of deep spiritual discernment: what Gregory described as the "art" of theological discourse, likening it to poetic insight that demanded a rigorous literary training (askesis) before it could be successfully navigated.

In regard to this study of the Book of Revelation, its doctrines and its reception in the larger community of the Eastern church, certain

---

50. He is alluding to Heb. 12:26-27; Hag. 2:6; Matt. 27:51.
51. John 14:26; 16:3. Gregory Nazianzen, *Orat.* 31.27.
52. Heb. 12:18.
53. Gregory Nazianzen, *Orat.* 31.25.

things appear to run like a current within the larger river, describing a certain shape of theological narrative which bears the mark of this central tradition. Let me try to summarize this in the following five concluding remarks. The first would seem to me to be the clear teaching that the church is itself the Eschatological Mystery. It is not an interim state, or a phenomenon of the interim between the eschatological promise of Parousial Judgment and the eventual fulfillment of that condition; rather it is the arena in which that promise is already being elaborated, qualified, and nuanced. This suggests the strange and ineffable role of the church as the locus of the holiness of the risen Lord in the present age. I am not arguing here that the church is the only locus of God's holiness or grace in the world, but intending to say something more specific: that the church is the holy of holies in the eschatological order, and the quality of its life of prayer, intercession, and charism is inextricably related to the eschaton. The heavenly liturgy of the eschaton, therefore, is not something that is yet to commence, but something that is already underway. Second, the Christian ethic clearly emerges as the mainspring of the church's eschatological awareness, and it will serve as the leaven to bring about the fulfillment of its eschatological calling in any generation. Third, and following from the previous point immediately, the failure of the church to live up to its high ethical calling serves to remind it that the fulfillment of its vocation to holiness can only be found in the merciful work of the Lord, not in its own record of achievements. The struggle for ethical purity, then, will be perfected only in the lively sense of repentance consequent on the acknowledgment of its "weakness of the flesh." In becoming a virtuoso of repentance the church learns how the finite stands before the Infinite, and becomes skilled in teaching a broken world about the "quality of mercy" — both its own and that of the Lord whom it manifests. In this, the church fulfills its fundamental eschatological duty to the world as laid upon it in Luke 24:47: the preaching of repentance for the forgiveness of sins. Fourth, the serious engagement with the struggle for ethical integrity leads inexorably in the life of any Christian, and in the church as a whole, to the profound sense that purity of heart can only be found in the mystery of love and communion it receives from the Spirit of God. The Christian ethic is something that is wholly based on the mystery of communion, and all other ethical motivations, even justice, faith, and hope themselves, will be subordinated to the eschatological communion in

the end, "when God will be all in all." This too is signified in the concept of the heavenly liturgy. The concept of the purity of heart and intention required of all the celebrants of the church's eucharistic liturgies is the symbol used from the earliest times to connote and
synthesize both concerns. And lastly, the whole tenor of the church's
eschatological sensibility seems to me to signify time and again that it
is only the assurance that the Lord is near, as savior and deliverer, that
could ever give the church the confidence or the eagerness (the ancient prayers spoke of *parrhesia* — the "reckless boldness") to cry out
in the words of that old Semitic pun with its double significance (at
once invocative and exclamative): Maranatha! Come Lord! — The
Lord is coming!

Luther and the Apocalypse:
Between Christ and History

PHILIP D. W. KREY

In the "Preface to the Prophet Isaiah" (1528) Luther writes that to understand this prophetic book one must "take in hand the last book of Kings and the last book of Chronicles and grasp them well, especially the events, the speeches, and the incidents that occurred under the kings named in the title [of Isaiah], clear to the end of those books. For if one would understand the prophecies, it is necessary that one know how things were in the land, how matters lay, what was in the mind of the people — what plans they had with respect to their neighbors, friends, and enemies — and especially what attitude they took in their country toward God and toward the prophet, whether they held to his word and worship or to idolatry."[1]

This is an affirmation by Luther of the importance of history and event in Scripture in the interpretation of prophecy. The writings of the prophets are not just "words and stories" but about "events and works."[2] To understand biblical prophetic works one must understand their history, context, and mentality.

At the conclusion of his "Preface to Daniel" in 1530, in which he details the history of Israel from Nebuchadnezzar to the Roman Em-

1. "Preface to the Prophet Isaiah" (1545 and 1528), in "Prefaces to the Old Testament," in *Luther's Works: Word and Sacrament* 1, vol. 35, ed. E. Theodore Bachmann (Philadelphia, 1960), p. 274.
2. See also "The Preface to the Prophets" (1532), "Prefaces to the Old Testament," p. 265.

pire, Luther emphasizes the christological themes in the prophets. As he writes in the "Preface to the Prophets," "For in the first place, the prophets proclaim and bear witness to the kingdom of Christ in which we now live. . . ."[3] Luther writes:

> For the prophecies of Daniel, and others like them, are not written simply that people may know history and the tribulations that are to come, and thus satisfy their curiosity, as with a news report, but in order that the righteous shall be encouraged and made joyful, and strengthened in faith and hope and patience. But here the righteous see and hear that their misery shall have an end, that they are to be freed from sins, death, the devil, and all evil — a freedom for which they yearn — and be brought to heaven, to Christ, into his blessed, everlasting kingdom. . . .
>
> Whoever would read them with profit must not depend entirely on the histories or stick exclusively to history, but rather refresh and comfort his heart with the promised and certain advent of our Savior Jesus Christ, who is the blessed and joyful redemption from this vale of misery and wretchedness.[4]

Although it is by no means new, Luther is keeping two streams of prophetic/apocalyptic interpretation together: the historical/prophetic and the evangelical and christological. History and the Christ of faith are held closely together.

Thus in the Daniel commentary of 1530 Luther is mildly scolding a part of the tradition that he thinks overly emphasized a historical reading of apocalyptic material.[5] In 1530 he sees that there is a closer

3. "Prefaces to the Old Testament," p. 265. The late-medieval exegete, Nicholas of Lyra, OFM (1270-1349), said the same thing about the prophets. He had claimed that while the prophets wrote about their own times their primary message was Jesus Christ. See the article by Frans van Liere in *Nicholas of Lyra: The Senses of Scripture*, ed. Philip Krey and Lesley Smith (Leiden, 2000).

4. The text also says: "This is how Christ too, in Luke 21[:28], comforts his own by means of the terrible news, saying, 'When you shall see these things, look up and raise your heads, because your redemption is near,' etc. For this reason we see that here too Daniel always ends all his visions and dreams, however terrible, with joy, namely, with Christ's kingdom and advent. It is on account of this advent, the last and most important thing, that these visions and dreams were given, interpreted, and written." "Preface to Daniel," in "Prefaces to the Old Testament," in *Word and Sacrament* 1, vol. 35, p. 316.

5. He may have been unfairly criticizing Nicholas of Lyra here, with whose works he was well acquainted. In 1329 Nicholas had commented on Daniel and Revelation by

connection between history and the expected advent of Christ, and, in fact, the end interprets that history. He now cautiously accepts apocalyptic writings in history as a prophetic interpretation of history. In other words, it is not by accident that in 1530 he devotes his Daniel preface to a detailed account of the history of the Jews in relation to their imperial oppressors and to the last judgment. Nonetheless, while acknowledging the importance of his own account (and those of his medieval predecessors) of Daniel's historical prophecies, he emphasizes the prophecy of the opponent of the gospel and of the promise of Christ and his judgment in Daniel.

It is well known, however, that Luther did not always recognize the validity of a close historical reading of apocalyptic material. In the 1522 "Preface to the Apocalypse" in the *September Testament* that will be cited below, he stressed the proclamation of Christ in the prophets that the Apocalypse seemed to lack, and he denounced the Book of Revelation. Here Luther's early reforming emphasis on the Christ of faith — the proclaimed Christ — is evident.

Heiko Oberman has taught us that one of Luther's significant achievements in his early religious breakthrough was to shift the late-medieval attention away from the fearful symmetry of the last judgment as the end to which all human earthly pilgrimages were tending, that is, the Judging Christ seated as in a medieval cathedral on the tympanum with the twenty-four elders seated round and the good and the damned rising or falling to either side.[6] This late-medieval apocalyptic view of the judging Christ collected around it the attendant attempts at religious appeasement. Luther pointed instead to the cross and resurrection as the judgment. Oberman's insight is made clear in a painting by Lucas Cranach the elder in the parish church at Wittenberg. Luther is in the pulpit pointing to the crucified Christ and he is centering the drama of the last judgment on the crucifixion/resurrection event. He follows a Johannine understanding of the crucifixion/resurrection/and ascension and last judgment as one event. In a similar altar piece by the older Cranach in the town church of St. Peter and Paul in Weimar, the Redeemer is lifted up on the cross with the victorious Lamb of the Apocalypse at the foot of the cross and the resur-

---

finding for the symbols and images of these prophetic and apocalyptic books exact historical referents.

6. Heiko Oberman, "'Iustitia Christi' and 'Iustia Dei': Luther and the Scholastic Doctrines of Justification," in *The Dawn of the Reformation* (Edinburgh, 1986), pp. 120-21.

rected Christ slaying death and the old Dragon alongside. The juxta-position of these eschatological themes is set in a medieval village context with John the Baptist pointing to the Crucified One and Lu-ther pointing to the open Scripture. Among the passages cited by the painter is John 3:14-15, "And as Moses lifted up the serpent in the wil-derness, even so must the son of man be lifted up, that whoever be-lieves in Him may have eternal life."[7]

In other words, contrary to the fourteenth-century depiction on the northern outside wall of the parish church of Wittenberg — in which the last judgment was understood as a final sorting before the Christ seated at the right hand of God — for Luther after his break-through, judgment was defined by the grace of the first advent in an-ticipation of the second. The same Christ would return for those who believe in him.[8]

Luther writes in 1522:

About this book of Revelation of John, I leave everyone free to hold his own opinions. I would not have anyone bound to my opinion or judgment. I say what I feel. I miss more than one thing in this book, and it makes me consider it to be neither apostolic nor prophetic.

First and foremost, the apostles do not deal with visions, but prophecy in clear and plain words, as do Peter and Paul, and Christ in the gospel. For it befits the apostolic office to speak clearly of Christ and his deeds, without images and visions. Moreover there is no prophet in the Old Testament, to say nothing of the New, who deals

7. Luther is also pointing in the open Bible to the last verse of chapter 4 of the Epistle to the Hebrews: "Let us then with confidence draw near to the throne of Grace, that we may receive mercy and find grace to help in time of need." In another example, Albrecht Dürer did not misunderstand his contemporary Luther or the Apocalypse when he followed his series on the Apocalypse including the famous four horsemen with a parallel series depicting the passion and resurrection of Christ. The passion se-ries is filled with the Reformation insights into the humanity of God — the compassion, the grace, and promise offered in the suffering, death, and resurrection of Jesus.

8. It is important to note, however, that Luther never lost the sense that there would also be a universal judgment and there would be confusion in history until then. His insight refers to the particular or individual's judgment. See also John 5:22-24. Moreover, although medieval iconography of the last judgment inspired fear and guilt, it was never without hope. See Bernard McGinn, "The Last Judgment in Christian Tra-dition," in *The Encyclopedia of Apocalypticism in Western History and Culture*, vol. 2, ed. Ber-nard McGinn (New York, 1998), pp. 394-95. See also the introduction to *Last Things: Death and the Apocalypse in the Middle Ages*, ed. Carolyn Walker Bynum and Paul Freed-man (Philadelphia, 2000), pp. 5-10.

so exclusively with visions and images. For myself, I think it approximates the Fourth Book of Esdras; I can in no way detect that the Holy Spirit produced it.

Moreover he seems to me to be going much too far when he commends his own book so highly [Revelation 22] — indeed, more than any of the other sacred books do, though they are much more important — and threatens that if anyone takes away anything from it, God will take away from him, etc. Again, they are supposed to be blessed who keep what is written in this book; and yet no one knows what that is, to say nothing of keeping it. This is just the same as if we did not have the book at all. And there are many other far better books available for us to keep.

Many of the fathers also rejected this book a long time ago; although St. Jerome, to be sure, refers to it in exalted terms and says that it is above all praise and that there are as many mysteries in it as words.[9] Still, Jerome cannot prove this at all, and his praise at numerous places is too generous.

Finally, let everyone think of it as his own spirit leads him. My spirit cannot accommodate itself to this book. For me this is reason enough not to think highly of it: Christ is neither taught nor known in it. But to teach Christ, this is the thing which an apostle is bound above all else to do; as Christ says in Acts 1[:8], "You shall be my witnesses." Therefore I stick to the books which present Christ to me clearly and purely.[10]

As described so well in Oberman's biography, Luther's lively doctrine of the Devil and the heritage of the Franciscan/Joachite interpretation of the Apocalypse that pervaded his mentality and context did not seem to affect this preface, which calls for a clear and literal proclamation of the gospel of Christ.[11] Luther had simply not yet experienced the power of evil in history or recognized the Reformation themes in the characters and symbols of apocalyptic literature. He missed the clear proclamation of Christ in the book. However, like many students of apocalyptic before and after, Luther's understanding of apocalyptic changed.

9. See Jerome's epistle *Ad Paulinum*, Migne PL 22, 548-49.

10. "Preface to the Revelation of St. John," in *Luther's Works*, pp. 398-99.

11. Heiko A. Oberman, *Mensch Zwischen Gott und Teufel* (Berlin, 1982), pp. 62-82. For a thorough analysis of this medieval apocalyptic tradition see vol. 2 of the *Encyclopedia of Apocalypticism* noted above.

In 1530, around the same time that he wrote his "Preface to Daniel," he would draw on the medieval historicizing resources available to him, and as always would recast them anew. Luther was a highly original apocalyptic interpreter.[12] The papacy's continued rejection of his reforms, the Peasants' War, and the threat of the Turkish conquest of Europe in addition to the dramatic confession before empire and church at Augsburg served as occasions for his apocalyptic sensitivities, which sharpened through much of his career.[13] As Robert Barnes comments, "Luther saw his own movement to revive the Gospel as the last great act in the great conflict between God and the Devil. God was allowing the light of truth to flash over the world with a final burst of clarity even as true believers were subjected to unprecedented threats and persecution."[14] The prophetic and apocalyptic writings in the Bible can now help to interpret God's actions in history and help to identify the forces of opposition. Like the passage with which I began from the "Preface to Daniel," also written in 1530, he sees the message of Revelation now to be one of consolation to suffering Christians in a historical context. Although he still seems skeptical about seeing God's revelation in history (I would even argue that he has rhetorical fun with the method), he plunges into the method popularized by the Franciscan Nicholas of Lyra (1270-1349) and its more radical adaptation by Wyclif.[15] He no longer objects to the images and figures of the book; instead he interprets them evangelically and historically/prophetically.

Now he writes in the "Preface to the Revelation" that will supplant the one of the *September Testament*: "Many have tried their hands [at interpreting this book], but until this very day they have attained no certainty. Some have even brewed it into many stupid things out of their own heads."[16] (Ironically the method he will adopt provides some bizarre historical associations for the great characters and fig-

---

12. Robert Barnes: "His reading of Scripture and his revision of prophetic truth became the key source of inspiration for a long tradition of Protestant apocalypticism." See "Images of Hope and Despair: Western Apocalypticism, ca. 1500-1800," in *The Encyclopedia of Apocalypticism in Western History and Culture*, p. 151.

13. See Jane Strohl, *Luther's Eschatology: The Last Times and the Last Things*, dissertation, University of Chicago (1989), pp. 228-33.

14. Barnes, "Images of Hope and Despair," p. 152.

15. See my article, "Many Readers but Few Followers: The Fate of Nicholas of Lyra's 'Apocalypse Commentary' in the Hands of His Late-Medieval Admirers," in *Church History* 64, no. 2 (June 1995): 185-201.

16. *LW*, vol. 35, p. 400.

ures of the Apocalypse — matching some of the popular associations today.) Luther continues,

> Because its interpretation is uncertain and its meaning hidden, we have also let it alone until now, especially because some of the ancient fathers held that it was not the work of St. John, the Apostle — as it is stated in *The Ecclesiastical History*, Book III, chapter 25.[17] For our part, we still share this doubt. By that, however, no one should be prevented from regarding this as the work of St. John the Apostle, or whomever else he chooses. Since we would nonetheless like to be sure of its meaning or interpretation, we will give other and higher minds something to think about by stating our own views.[18]

Luther proceeds to adapt a method popularized by the Franciscan Nicholas of Lyra.[19]

This should not be surprising, since, famous for the literal/historical interpretation of the Bible and sometimes called the second Jerome, Nicholas, through his *Apocalypse Commentary*, is reputed to have influenced late-medieval commentators to Luther and the Reformation and beyond. Writing and publishing two complete biblical commentaries over his long tenure as a Franciscan administrator in Paris, he became an immediate authority as an exegete in the printings of the Vulgate with the *Glossa ordinaria*.[20] Nicholas popularized a method that was later used because it was straightforward and based on a literal interpretation that was gaining acceptance in the late Middle Ages, but his better judgments were widely ignored, especially by Luther and his proximate sources, with significant consequences for the history of Apocalypse interpretation.[21] As I have said, Luther adapted Lyra's method but drew from the Wycliffite and Radi-

17. Eusebius, *History* 3.25.2-4.

18. LW, 35, 400.

19. See Bernard McGinn, "Revelation," in *The Literary Guide to the Bible*, ed. Robert Alter and Frank Kermode (Cambridge, Mass., 1987), p. 534.

20. See the excellent discussion by Karlfried Froehlich of how Nicholas's works came into the printings of the Gloss in the Introduction to the Facsimile Reprint of the *Editio Princeps, Biblia Latina Cum Glossa ordinaria, Adolph Rusch of Strassburg 1480/81*, ed. Karlfried Froehlich and Margaret T. Gibson (Turnhout, Belgium: Brepols, 1992), pp. xvif.

21. Lyra always cloaked his criticisms with one of two favorite phrases, "salvo meliori judicio videtur mihi" (without prejudice to better judgment it seems to me) or "salva reverentia videtur" (with all due respect, it seems), indicating that he was willing to subject himself to future, more correct opinions and also attempting something new.

cal Franciscan traditions.[22] These traditions historicized the Apocalypse but were quick to identify their own time and their contemporaries — especially ecclesiastical figures — with the Antichrist. Luther likewise takes an obligatory run through church history and then jumps to what he really wants to address, namely, current events and the presence of the Antichrist in those events.

Luther writes in the 1530 preface: "Since it is intended as a revelation of things that are to happen in the future, and especially of tribulations and disasters that were to come upon Christendom, we consider that the first and surest step toward finding its interpretation is to take from history the events and disasters that have come upon Christendom till now, and hold them up alongside these images, and so compare them very carefully. If, then, the two perfectly coincided and squared with one another, we could build on that as a sure, or at least an unobjectionable, interpretation."[23]

Like his predecessors Luther marches through the book making correlations but in a way that is free and more like Wyclif than Lyra. He contends that the seven letters are real letters to the seven churches of Asia and then proceeds to narrate history beginning in the eighth chapter. The angel of the seal of the living God represents good theologians and preachers with whom the church is always blessed. Among the examples he provides are Athanasius and Hilary of Poitiers. As Jaroslav Pelikan has shown, Luther's agenda become clear in the eighth chapter.[24] His interest is more dogmatic than historical, more evangelical than exegetical. In the vision of the angels with the trumpets, every evil angel is opposed to a Reformation principle. The first bad angel is Tatian, the second-century ascetic who forbade marriage; to Luther he is a prime example of works righteousness. Works righteousness, he writes, had to be the first doctrine against the gospel, and it also remains the last, except that it is always getting new teachers and new names, such as Pelagius.[25] The second angel with

22. Luther also employs and adapts to his purposes the linear-historical method in his 1530 commentary on the Apocalypse. See note 14 above.

23. *LW*, vol. 35, p. 401. This is precisely the way Nicholas and Wyclif described their methods.

24. Jaroslav Pelikan, "Some Uses of the Apocalypse in the Magisterial Reformers," in *The Apocalypse in English Renaissance Thought and Literature,* ed. C. A. Patrides and Joseph Wittreich (Ithaca, N.Y., 1984), p. 81.

25. *LW*, vol. 35, p. 402.

the trumpet is Marcion, the Manichaeans and the Montanists, who "extol their own spirituality above all the Scriptures," as do "Münzer and the fanatics in our day."[26] Here Luther objects to those who offer a private spiritual interpretation.

Like Wyclif, Luther is most concerned with the current condition of the gospel's proclamation. The third angel with the trumpet (8:10, 11) is Origen, who "embittered and corrupted the Scriptures with philosophy and reason, as the universities have hitherto done among us." These are those, he notes, who cannot accept the scandal and foolishness of the gospel. The fourth bad angel is Novatus, the fourth-century rigorist, and more importantly the Donatists who obviously reject the Reformation and its doctrine of *simul justus et peccator*.[27]

At this point Luther writes, "The scholars who know history will know how to reckon this out, for it would take too long to relate and prove everything."[28] (Luther is having fun now.) Interpreting the first woe in chapter 9, Luther says the fifth angel is "the great heretic Arius and his companions. . . . For they presecuted the true Christians not only spiritually but physically, with the sword. Read the history of the Arians, and then you will understand this figure and these words." The sixth angel and the second woe is Muhammad, and the angel accompanying this woe the one with the rainbow over his head is the holy papacy and holding the scroll is the great spiritual show. The mother and child of chapter 12 represent the church that endures in spite of the Dragon's attack. The two witnesses of chapter 11 represent the good preaching of the gospel throughout the history of the church.[29]

With the beasts in chapter 13, Luther is deeply into his current conflicts and identifies the two as the papal empire and the imperial papacy. The church before the "imperial papacy" and the church afterwards represent the two periods of church for Luther.[30] Luther writes, "The abominations, woes, and injuries which this imperial papacy has wrought cannot now be recounted. For [through it] the world has been filled with all kinds of idolatry — with monasteries, foundations, saints, pilgrimages, purgatory, indulgences, celibacy, and innumerable

26. *LW,* vol. 35, pp. 402-3.
27. *LW,* vol. 35, p. 403.
28. *LW,* vol. 35, p. 404.
29. *LW,* vol. 35, pp. 404-5.
30. See John M. Headley, *Luther's View of Church History* (New Haven, 1963), pp. 181-94, and esp. 194.

other articles of human doctrine and works, etc." And "who can re-count how much bloodshed . . . and misery the popes have wrought, both by themselves fighting and by stirring up the emperors, kings, and princes against one another?"[31]

It is important to note at this point that Luther's identification of the papacy as Antichrist became part of the Smalcaldic Articles and was fateful for Lutheran propaganda.[32] Luther identified the institu-tion of the papacy itself as the incarnation of the corrupted gospel. Lu-ther could have learned more from the more moderate Franciscan apocalyptic tradition represented by Lyra and less from the radical Franciscan and Wycliffite traditions.[33] Nevertheless, it indicates how Luther perceived his own time to be the occasion for the apocalyptic struggle between God and Satan, and his own proclamation of the gospel was the flashpoint. The fight was out in the open; therefore a defensive apocalyptic expectancy.

On a comic note, in chapter 16, Luther sees the frogs as Faber, Eck, and Emser, Luther's opponents, "who croak much against the gospel, accomplish nothing and remain frogs."[34] In summary, the con-clusion to the preface states that the Book of Revelation is really about consolation for the suffering saints. Luther also takes great consola-tion in the fact that the church has always had internal and external challenges; thus it too is an article of faith. It is not yet what it will be:

> Some of the know-it-alls are even now doing that very thing. They see heresy and dissension and shortcomings of many kinds; they see that there are many false, many loose-living Christians. And so they de-cide offhand that there are no Christians anywhere. . . .
>
> They ought to read this book and learn to look upon Christen-dom with other eyes than those of reason. For this book, I think, shows plenty of gruesome and monstrous beasts, horrible and vindic-

---

31. *LW,* vol. 35, p. 406.

32. See Pelikan, "Some Uses of the Apocalypse," p. 86. Luther writes in these arti-cles (1537), "This is a powerful demonstration that the pope is the real Antichrist who has raised himself over and set himself against Christ, for the pope will not permit Christians to be saved except by his own power, which amounts to nothing since it is neither established nor commanded by God." *Smalcaldic Articles,* Part 2, Article 4, in *The Book of Concord,* ed. Theodore Tappert (Philadelphia, 1959), p. 300.

33. Nicholas had refused to see Antichrist as a historical figure within the church as the radical Franciscans had done.

34. *LW,* vol. 35, pp. 407-8.

tive angels, . . . (not to speak of the other great faults and shortcomings that have always been in Christendom and among Christians) so that in the midst of such business natural reason necessarily had to lose [sight of] Christendom. Here we see clearly what ghastly offenses and shortcomings there have been prior to our times, when Christendom is thought to have been at its best. By comparison, ours is really a golden age. . . .

This article, "I believe in the holy Christian Church," is as much an article of faith as the rest. . . .

[L]et them do what they can! If only the word of the gospel remains pure among us, and we love and cherish it, we shall not doubt that Christ is with us, even when things are at their worst. . . . Christ is nonetheless with his saints, and wins the final victory.[35]

There is a concrete promise in the expectation of a last judgment, but the judgment has already occurred in the cross and resurrection that Luther now sees as the center of the Apocalypse via the doctrine of justification by faith. Thus all of the good and the monstrous figures and events of history are relativized by the crucifixion/resurrection and the church's evangelical and historical role in the final advent. Nevertheless, Luther's insistence on the historical manifestation of Antichrist in the papacy of his time weakens his consoling message and focuses the Protestant tradition's attention away from Christ and his first and second advents. Would that he had respected the more sober voices about the Antichrist in the church represented by Nicholas of Lyra and other moderate voices. Nevertheless, the very purpose of his "Preface to the Revelation" in 1530 is to balance historical event and evangelical hope, and Luther's apocalyptic hope transcends the defeats of his Reformation's causes. History's contradictions and his hope in the power of the gospel were at the center of his apocalypticism. To put it in his own words from the "Preface to Daniel," "The writings of the prophets are not just 'words and stories' but about 'events and works.'" Christ must be proclaimed with confidence in the face of history's advances and failures.

---

35. *LW*, vol. 35, p. 411. See Headley, *Luther's View of Church History*, pp. 181-94, and esp. 194. See also Strohl, *Luther's Eschatology*, pp. 1-16.

Hints from Science for Eschatology — and Vice Versa

GEORGE L. MURPHY

Introduction

Eschatology is oriented toward the future, though it is not just about the future. Human intelligence with its abilities to recognize regularities in the world and extrapolate from them makes it possible for us to estimate more or less precisely what some aspects of the future will be. Thus it is not surprising that attempts to explore the Christian vision of the eschaton often have appealed to the current state of knowledge of the natural world and natural processes. In the sixth century John Philoponus, in debate with the pagan Proclus, argued for inherent destructibility of the world on the basis of the Platonic and Aristotelian physics of the time.[1] A century ago, with a somewhat better understanding of the world, scientists speculated about a "heat death of

---

1. Seymour Feldman, "The End of the Universe: A Medieval Debate" in David Novak and Norbert Samuelson, eds., *Creation and the End of Days* (Lanham, Md.: University Press of America, 1986), pp. 215-44.

Much of the work on this paper was done while I was a Visiting Scholar at the Center for Theology and the Natural Sciences of the Graduate Theological Union in Berkeley, for whose hospitality I am thankful. Study leave support was provided by St. Mark Lutheran Church in Tallmadge, Ohio. I appreciate especially the encouragement in this work from Professor Robert John Russell, the Director of the Center, and numerous conversations with him.

the universe" on the basis of the Second Law of Thermodynamics.[2] While a Christian like Philoponus could see the wearing out of the universe in the light of a hope for new heavens and a new earth, the heat death was usually spoken of as something to be feared. New developments in physics have shown the tentative character of those scientific predictions.

But the tentative character of science doesn't mean we should not try to make predictions. Science really does enable us to understand the world to some degree. So we pose the question: What can the natural sciences suggest — not tell us with certainty but suggest — about the future of the universe that may be helpful for Christian eschatology? And we can also go the other way and ask whether that Christian vision might suggest areas that science might find it profitable to investigate.

Eschatological Ambiguities

When we look at all the ways in which the Bible and Christian tradition have spoken about the Last Things, we find that there are a number of ambiguities or tensions between apparently opposite poles, both of which must be given adequate attention. It is of course easiest and most comfortable simply to eliminate these ambiguities, but only at the cost of dropping important aspects of the biblical witness. When we respect the ambiguities, and in good Lutheran fashion are willing to live with paradox, they suggest that we should be able to use current scientific knowledge in order to see some connections between the present world and the eschaton, but that we should not expect to encompass the fullness of God's purpose for the world within a framework of natural science.

The first of these ambiguities is the familiar one of realized and future eschatologies, the tension between the "now" and the "not yet." Christians live in the tension between the present eon and the age to come. The fulfillment of God's promise for the world has begun, but it is not yet finished. Believers "have been raised with

---

2. Erwin N. Hiebert, "Modern Science and Christian Faith," in *God and Nature*, ed. David C. Lindberg and Ronald L. Numbers (Berkeley: University of California Press, 1986), pp. 425-27.

Christ" (Col. 3:1) and "have tasted . . . the powers of the age to come" (Heb. 6:5), but are warned against those "who have swerved from the truth by claiming that the resurrection has already taken place" (2 Tim. 2:18). A realized eschatology seems very clear in the Gospel of John, where Christ says that the individual believer "has eternal life, and does not come under judgment, but has passed from death to life" (John 5:24). But a few verses later there is also a statement about the future, that "the hour is coming when all who are in their graves will hear his voice, and will come out" (John 5:28-29).

"If anyone is in Christ, there is a new creation: everything old has passed away; see, everything has become new!" (2 Cor. 5:17). Paul is speaking about the present and seems to see this "new creation" as something completely separate from the old. In the Book of Revelation the seer's final vision of the culmination of God's works expands this idea of new creation from the individual Christian to cosmos: "Then I saw a new heaven and a new earth; for the first earth had passed away, and the sea was no more" (Rev. 21:1). This echoes the language of new heavens and earth found elsewhere in Scripture, in Isaiah (65:17; 66:22) and 2 Peter (3:13). But we have here another ambiguity, for this new creation is a *heaven and earth*, a transformation of our present world, and not simply an annihilation of the present order of things and its replacement by some reality of a completely different kind. As we read on in the description of the holy city, New Jerusalem, it becomes clear that the previous creation has not just been abolished.[3] "The kings of the earth will bring their glory into [the city]. . . . People will bring into it the glory and the honor of the nations" (Rev. 21:24, 26). The glory and honor of the nations must be the good that has been accomplished in the course of world history: The next verse (v. 27) says that the unclean and those who practice abomination will be excluded. Those who are especially important in bringing this glory into the holy city are "the kings of the earth" — who throughout the book have been the enemies of God's people.

New creation does not mean simple annihilation of the old, which God saw as "very good" in Genesis (1:31). And while the new creation breaks in abruptly — "We will all be changed, in a moment, in the twinkling of an eye, at the last trumpet" (1 Cor. 15:51-52) — it is

---

3. G. B. Caird, *The Revelation of St. John the Divine* (New York: Harper & Row, 1966), pp. 279-80.

rooted in the old: A few verses before that "twinkling of an eye" phrase Paul uses the image of a continuous process, the growing of a seed into a plant, to speak of the resurrection of the dead. And of course that hope of the resurrection is founded on the new creation *par excellence*, the raising of Jesus of Nazareth who walked the old earth and whose roots the Gospel writers trace back through the history of Israel.

The "new heaven and a new earth" are then not completely disjoined from the present heaven and earth. This final act will take place in a discontinuous manner, and there will be an abrupt change from mortality to imperishability, but it will preserve all that is good of the old, and in some way is made possible through the old.

These tensions, between the now and the not yet, old and new, continuity and discontinuity, are related because the creation of the genuinely new is the future. Pannenberg's statement is well known: "If Jesus has been raised, then the end of the world has begun."[4] The resurrection of Jesus in the middle of history is a prolepsis of the eschaton, God's ultimate future coming into the now *from* the future, the new breaking into the old. Ted Peters has developed a systematic theology around the theme of prolepsis, "the invasion of the present by the power of what is yet to come." The future is not merely *futurum*, the future as it unfolds causally from the past, or even *adventus*, the future as bringing something absolutely new, but also *venturum*, the future as it "has an impact on us before its full advent."[5] We can say that the new creation takes place from the future.

But God's eschatological work is also, as John Polkinghorne puts it, *creatio ex vetere*, creation from the old: "[T]he new creation is the divine redemption of the old."[6] God does not simply dispense with the first creation. It is Jesus of Nazareth, a human being sharing in the life of the historical people of Israel (Matt. 1:1-17) and the death that is the common lot of humanity in the present world, who is risen to be the focus of eschatological hope. The element of continuity between the historical Jesus and the risen Christ means that the picture of Je-

4. Wolfhart Pannenberg, *Jesus — God and Man*, 2nd ed. (Philadelphia: Westminster, 1977), p. 67.

5. Ted Peters, *GOD — The World's Future* (Minneapolis: Fortress Press, 1992), esp. pp. 308-9.

6. John Polkinghorne, *The Faith of a Physicist* (Princeton, N.J.: Princeton University Press, 1994), p. 167.

sus in the Gospels gives us a look at what God's ultimate future for the universe will be like.

If we are to take seriously the element of continuity in eschatology and to understand the eschaton as *ex vetere*, we have to consider what science can suggest to us about the future on the basis of our current understanding of the world. That is one of the primary things that scientific laws are supposed to do — establish connections between a present state of affairs and the future state, even if that connection has only a statistical character, as in quantum theory.

If the future develops out of the present, however, we naturally ask how anything genuinely new, anything not already potentially present in the old, can arise. That question of how there can be anything new is more fundamental than any questions we may have about the predictions of specific evolutionary or cosmological theories. The belief that new creation is from the future suggests a radically different way of looking at the connections between events. Scientific views of the future can, and in some cases must, help to inform our theology. But theology, in turn, will enable us to suggest both some lines of scientific research that might be fruitful and some limits to the applicability of science. The next thing we need to do here is to review briefly what science does suggest about the far future of the cosmos and life within it.

The Future in Scientific Cosmology

When Einstein first applied his new concept of gravitation, the general theory of relativity, to cosmology in 1917, he accepted the general scientific thinking of the time that the physical universe as a whole was eternal and unchanging.[7] It was realized that stars move relative to one another, and the Second Law of Thermodynamics had, as we already noted, led some theologians, as well as scientists, to think about a possible "heat death of the universe." But the physical configuration of the universe was thought of as changeless. It is worth noting that Einstein may have been influenced as much by religious belief as by astronomical observations. Throughout his life he was a great admirer

---

7. For the history of scientific cosmology to the mid-1950s see J. D. North, *The Measure of the Universe* (New York: Dover, 1990).

of Spinoza, and Max Jammer suggests in his recent book *Einstein and Religion* that Spinoza's statement in his *Ethics* of the immutability of God and all his attributes would suggest for a pantheist that the universe also should be immutable.[8]

Einstein realized that his theory, which explains gravitation in terms of the curvature of space-time, introduced the possibility of a universe that was finite in size but unbounded, like the three-dimensional surface of a four-dimensional sphere. But it seemed that such a universe could not be static, for gravitational attraction would make it collapse. Einstein circumvented this difficulty by adding what came to be called a "cosmological term" to his equations. This amounted to adding a new *repulsive* force, which would grow larger with distance, to the ordinary attractive gravitational force. Cosmological repulsion could balance gravitational attraction, making possible a finite and static universe.

New observational and theoretical work soon overtook Einstein's model. Hubble's correlation of shifts in galactic spectra with distances showed that the universe was not static but expanding, and theoretical work by de Sitter, Friedmann, Lemaître, and Robertson had discovered solutions of Einstein's equations, both with and without the cosmological term, representing universes that expanded or contracted in the course of time. It was quickly realized that some of these model universes might represent the world of galaxies that Hubble's work disclosed.[9]

For our purposes attention can be limited to the simplest model universes in which matter is distributed uniformly and in which an observer at any point would see the same thing in any direction. (This seems to be true in an average sense for our universe.) There are then three possibilities for the spatial geometry of the world. Einstein's universe is a three-dimensional space with constant *positive* curvature

8. Max Jammer, *Einstein and Religion* (Princeton, N.J.: Princeton University Press, 1999), p. 62.

9. The term "model universe" of G. C. McVittie, *General Relativity and Cosmology,* 2nd ed. (Urbana, Ill.: University of Illinois Press, 1965), ch. 8, should be noted. Theorists have studied many cosmological solutions of Einstein's equations, some of which have features like our universe, while others have surprising properties and bear little resemblance to the universe we inhabit. The model proposed by Hartle and Hawking in which the universe has no temporal beginning but "just is" has intriguing theoretical features but has not yet been shown to be capable of representing our universe in any detail. For a popular account see Stephen W. Hawking, *A Brief History of Time* (New York: Bantam, 1988), ch. 8.

and finite volume. There can also be spaces with constant *negative* curvature, which would be infinite in extent. Finally, a flat space with *zero* curvature, in which the familiar geometry of Euclid would obtain, would also be infinite.[10]

All of these models can expand in the course of time, and thus accommodate Hubble's discovery. Interest in them over the past seventy years has concentrated on what they can tell us about the past, in part because this might allow us to make some connection with religious beliefs about creation. If cosmic expansion is extrapolated back in time, the universe at earlier epochs would have been in states of higher temperature and density, and these variables grow without bounds as we approach the beginning of the expansion. Current observations indicate that this expansion did in fact begin in such a hot, dense state, the "big bang," something like thirteen billion years ago.

We are concerned here, however, with the future of the universe. The behaviors of our models in the course of time can be described by analogy with what happens when a rocket is shot outward from the earth. The closed model with positive curvature is like a rocket given a velocity *less* than escape velocity, which will slow down, stop, and fall back to earth. Expansion of this model universe will eventually halt and contraction will ensue: A universe that began in a "big bang" will end in a "big crunch," in which density and temperature will grow beyond all bounds. The model with constant negative curvature, on the other hand, is like a rocket given *more* than escape velocity, which will continue to move outward forever, though with decreasing speed. The corresponding model universe will expand forever. Flat space is like the rocket given precisely escape velocity. It will also expand forever, but at a rate approaching zero in the far future. In the latter two models, matter will continually cool and thin out as the expansion proceeds.

Models are multiplied if we admit the cosmological term. But except for Einstein's original solution, which has been found to be unstable, the long-term prospects for the universe are still those described above, either a "big crunch" or expansion that continues forever. These have been described as "fry" and "freeze" scenarios be-

10. Models with negative or zero curvature can also be made finite by giving them different topologies. See, e.g., Jean-Pierre Luminet et al., "Is Space Finite?" *Scientific American* 280, no. 4 (1999): 90.

cause the temperature of matter and radiation in the first case would increase without limit as the universe contracted, and in the second case would drop inexorably toward absolute zero. Neither possibility seems to offer much room for the traditional eschatological images of Christian theology, or indeed of any afterlife that has some connection with the physical world. How could any sort of life exist if temperatures approach either infinity or zero?

Closer examination shows, however, that the situation is not entirely desperate. One thing that is crucial for meaningful human life is the capacity for reason and moral judgment, made possible by our intelligence. But intelligence may not be unique to us among physical entities. Many scientists today believe that artificial intelligence is possible in principle,[11] and if that is the case it would be possible for minds to be run on hardware quite different from that of our brains. It is conceivable that computers could be developed that would be able to exist and process information under physical conditions our present bodies could not survive. While our biological descendants might not be able to live under future conditions in the universe, perhaps our machine descendants could.

Analysis of how such computers might function reveals a surprising fact: There are model universes of both the "freeze" and the "fry" variety in which an infinite amount of new information could, in theory, be processed.[12] Some artificial intelligence units, perhaps operating at the level of elementary particles, would be able to think an infinite number of new thoughts, and in this sense would be able to "live forever."

That is perhaps not too surprising for the ever-expanding model universes. It is true that the speed of information processing decreases as the temperature drops, so that it takes more time to process a given number of bits, but there is unlimited time available in these models. Analysis shows that in some cases this unlimited time can make up for a processing rate that approaches zero. But this can also work in some models with a big crunch, which in the usual sense have only a finite time available. In this case the extremely high tempera-

11. For views on this pro and con see, respectively, Douglas R. Hofstadter, *Gödel, Escher, Bach: An Eternal Golden Braid* (New York: Basic Books, 1979), and Roger Penrose, *The Emperor's New Mind* (New York: Oxford University Press, 1989).

12. John D. Barrow and Frank J. Tipler, *The Anthropic Cosmological Principle* (New York: Oxford University Press, 1986), ch. 10.

tures may make possible a rate of information processing that grows without bounds as infinite compression is approached. Again, analysis shows that it may be possible for an infinite number of bits to be processed.

Model universes are interesting, but what about the real world we inhabit? Ever since Hubble announced his discovery of the recession of galaxies in 1929, cosmologists have been trying to find which, if any, of the models provided by Einstein's theory represents our universe accurately. It is difficult to answer this question for a number of reasons. One of the most serious problems is the difficulty of making accurate measurements of the distances of galaxies billions of light years away, where the differences between various models would be discernible. The weight of opinion of cosmologists has swung back and forth over the past seventy years, and a knowledge of that history should make us wary of endorsing any claims in the matter as definitive.

With due reticence, then, we can point to the convergence of several recent investigations which indicate that the universe is either flat or negatively curved, and thus will expand forever. Perhaps more surprising is the fact that the cosmic expansion does not seem to be slowing down due to gravitational attraction, but appears to be *accelerating*.[13] The simplest way to explain this result is with the cosmological constant that Einstein originally introduced to make a static universe possible. When the recession of the galaxies was discovered, Einstein rejected this term and called it his "greatest blunder,"[14] and many physicists have wanted to follow him and ignore the cosmological term. But there are other theoretical approaches, some unrelated to cosmological problems, which indicate that this term should be retained in the gravitational field equations. If the present observational results continue to hold good, then physicists will have to come to terms with what may have been a quite serendipitous blunder.

---

13. Several articles in *Scientific American* 280, no. 1 (January 1999), are devoted to aspects of these results.

14. George Gamow, *My World Line* (New York: Viking, 1970), p. 44.

Approaches to Eschatology

There has been considerable theological interest in eschatology in recent years, but a great deal of the work that has been done in this area has given no attention to what scientific cosmology tells us about the future evolution of the universe.[15] If one is not content with a completely spiritualized eschatology that has no connection with the present physical universe, an approach that ignores the scientific ideas described in the previous section must depend, explicitly or implicitly, on a miraculous intervention by God to bring about the kingdom. Of course that can be defended with an appeal to divine omnipotence: "Is anything too wonderful for the LORD?" (Gen. 18:14). God can do something that is completely unforeseen by current science. But this "It's a miracle" approach means a complete lack of continuity between the present order of things and the new creation. The old contributes nothing to the new. The old earth has passed away but the glory and honor of the nations have not been brought into the New Jerusalem.

At the other extreme, some physicists in recent years[16] have tried to develop purely scientific understandings of the far future, and have presented them as pictures of the ultimate state of the cosmos. This is done by assuming the validity of the best current theories of physics and using them to extrapolate the present state of the known universe as far as possible into the future. The possibilities that these futures may hold for physical life in the broadest possible sense, including artificial intelligence and its spread through the cosmos, can then be discussed. These theories intend to be purely scientific, and they avoid any input from revelation. They can, in spite of that, be seen as secularized versions of Christian eschatology, similar to the status of Marx's "scientific socialism."[17] The fact that Marx's grand vision has

15. Some earlier attempts to relate science and Christian eschatology are discussed in Hans Schwarz, *On the Way to the Future*, rev. ed. (Minneapolis: Augsburg, 1979), ch. 4. A more recent discussion that addresses some of the issues set out in the previous section is Mark William Worthing, *God, Creation, and Contemporary Physics* (Minneapolis: Fortress Press, 1996), ch. 5.

16. F. J. Dyson, "Time Without End: Physics and Biology in an Open Universe," *Reviews of Modern Physics* 51 (1979): 447; Jamal N. Islam, *The Ultimate Fate of the Universe* (Cambridge: Cambridge University Press, 1983); Barrow and Tipler, *The Anthropic Cosmological Principle*, ch. 10. Frank J. Tipler, *The Physics of Immortality* (New York: Doubleday, 1994); Paul Davies, *The Last Three Minutes* (New York: Basic Books, 1994).

17. Schwarz, *On the Way to the Future*, pp. 144-52.

not been fulfilled of course does not in itself discredit all such attempts.

The most ambitious and controversial of these "scientific eschatologies" is Frank Tipler's.[18] He argues that in a closed universe our machine descendants could populate the entire universe and alter cosmic evolution to bring about a type of big crunch in which infinite information processing could occur. It is necessary to engineer this crunch so that the rate of contraction varies from one direction to another, thus producing a temperature differential on which the machines can run. Talk of "engineering" the collapse of the universe indicates how grandiose this vision is, but its author goes to some lengths to show that it violates none of our present laws of physics.

The future causal boundary of this universe is an "Omega Point" whose name (but, says Tipler, nothing else in the theory) comes from Teilhard de Chardin.[19] Tipler identifies this with God. Since this God has unlimited information processing capacity it can run the programs of all entities who have ever lived in a perfect virtual reality which is the resurrection.

Tipler's theory is worked out in greater detail than other scientific eschatologies, but shares with them some general defects to be discussed below. In addition, the recent cosmological observations to which I've referred indicate that our universe is not of the type this theory requires: There apparently will be continued expansion rather than a big crunch. There is also a serious theological objection to Tipler's picture. His is a theory of resurrection without the cross, a pure theology of glory. For those who agree with Luther that "true theology and recognition of God are in the crucified Christ,"[20] this is fatal.

This does not mean that Tipler's work is of no theological value. I think it is important to emphasize this, because Tipler has received a lot of unfair comment and ridicule in addition to legitimate criticism.[21] We cannot accept his totalizing claim to make theology a branch of

18. Tipler, *The Physics of Immortality*.

19. Tipler, *The Physics of Immortality*, p. 110.

20. "Heidelberg Disputation," in *Luther's Works*, vol. 31 (Philadelphia: Fortress Press, 1957), p. 53.

21. See, e.g., the reviews of *The Physics of Immortality* by Joseph I. Silk, *Scientific American* 273, no. 1 (1995): 93, by Donald G. York and Hans-Dieter Mutschler in *Zygon* 30 (1995): 477 and 479 respectively, and by George L. Murphy, *dialog* 34 (1995): 236.

physics, but some of his individual ideas may be useful to theologians as a resource for their own work.

Purely scientific visions of the future avoid the fundamental eschatological ambiguities by removing the elements of newness and discontinuity. Nothing radically different can emerge. This does not mean just that they deny the possibility of divine intervention. They also implicitly assume that no fundamental scientific or technological discoveries will be made in the future. They not only emphasize the "now" but assume that our present theories or predictable extensions of them enable us to understand all phenomena that may be relevant for the evolution of life and the universe. These attempts at scientific eschatology are sometimes dismissed as "science fiction," but it is significant that none of them envisions the possibility of a fundamental breakthrough in physics that would make possible some type of faster-than-light travel and the interstellar communications common in science fiction: There will be no starship *Enterprise* or *Millennium Falcon* in Tipler's universe. The possibility that such a discovery might render obsolete the slow sub-light creep of ships bearing self-reproducing von Neumann machines across the universe is never envisioned. As we will see, the development of genuine faster-than-light travel would necessitate basic changes in the ways we think about the relationships between past, present, and future.

An adequate treatment of eschatology today must avoid both extremes, that of ignoring science and that of relying entirely on extrapolation of today's science. We need to take into account what science tells us about the universe and its predictions for the future, and try to gain some insights into the possibilities for divine transformation of the world in the present order of things. But we also have to be open to the possibility of something qualitatively new.

Temporal Order and Causality in the Universe

The apparent acceleration of cosmic expansion can be explained most simply with the cosmological term that Einstein added to his equations, for the repulsive force this represents has just the desired effect. This cosmological term has a definite structure, and produces physical effects identical with those of a material medium filling all of space. It would have the same density of energy at every point of space, and a very large *negative* pressure.

Negative pressure in a material means that it is under tension, like a stretched rope. While it seems odd for a fluid to be in such a condition, this situation does occur: Water is drawn to the tops of trees by negative pressure in their sap.[22] But there the magnitude of the pressure is very small in comparison with the density of energy of the mass involved ($E = mc^2$), while the cosmological term represents a negative pressure and density of energy that are equal in magnitude. Negative pressure means that the medium does negative work as it expands so that its energy increases by just the right amount to keep the density of energy constant. Thus it would keep the same density, without thinning out, as the universe expanded.[23]

This sounds strange, but it is not as surprising as another feature of a material with such properties. Its properties violate the formal mathematical conditions that restrict waves in a fluid to speeds less than that of light. This does not violate the basic requirements of relativity, for the speed of light is still the same for all observers, but it is no longer an upper limit on attainable speeds. It is known in relativity theory that a body which could move faster than light would be able to reverse the direction of its motion in time. Consequently, a material with the properties similar to that of the cosmological term might make possible the sending of signals backward in time.[24]

Since these ideas are unusual we should note that they are not unprecedented. Before he gave up on the cosmological term, Einstein tried to use the negative pressure it implies to explain the stability of the basic particles of matter. In 1968 the Soviet theorist Ya. B. Zel'dovich pointed out that the energy which quantum field theory attributes to the vacuum has properties like those of Einstein's cosmological term.[25]

But what about the idea of signals traveling backward in time? We certainly do not receive messages from the future or encounter time

22. Alan H. Cromer, *Physics for the Life Sciences*, 2nd ed. (New York: McGraw-Hill, 1977), pp. 201-3.

23. W. H. McCrea, "Relativity Theory and the Creation of Matter," *Proceedings of the Royal Society* A206 (1951): 562.

24. S. W. Hawking and G. F. R. Ellis, *The Large Scale Structure of Space-Time* (New York: Cambridge University Press, 1973), pp. 88-96.

25. Albert Einstein, *The Meaning of Relativity*, 5th ed. (Princeton, N.J.: Princeton University, 1955), p. 106. (This material is from the first edition of 1922.); Ya. B. Zel'dovich, "The Cosmological Constant and the Theory of Elementary Particles," *Soviet Physics Uspekhi* 11 (1968): 381.

travelers in the way that inhabitants of some science fiction worlds do. The possibility of such effects has, however, long been known to physicists.[26] Radio waves traveling at the speed of light would take about four hours to get to earth from a spacecraft near Neptune: Reception of the signal is "retarded" with respect to its sending. This seems now to be just common sense. But the equations of electromagnetic theory describe not only such "retarded" waves, but also *advanced* waves that would be received four hours *before* the signal was sent! Advanced waves propagate backward in time just as retarded waves propagate forward. Physicists usually ignore the advanced wave solutions, but some have tried to use them to solve problems on the level of elementary particles without introducing any anomalous effects on the macroscopic level. We either ignore these solutions or try to limit their role only because of criteria we impose on the theory from outside. There is no logical reason within electromagnetic theory itself to prefer retarded over advanced waves. The theory is symmetric between past and future.

This is not the only way in which phenomena violating our conventional sense of time ordering might occur. Over fifty years ago Kurt Gödel found a solution of Einstein's equations in which there are "closed time-like world lines," which means that some observers, without exceeding the speed of light, could get into their own pasts.[27] Other "time machine" solutions of Einstein's equations have been found, and the suggestion that time travel might be facilitated by wormholes held open by "exotic matter" has received serious consideration in recent years.[28] While such phenomena are still very speculative, they are no longer limited to science fiction.

If signals, and even material objects, can move backward in time then some radical changes in our ways of looking at the world are needed. The past is no longer "the dead past" but is accessible to observers in the future. Clearly there must be some requirements of consistency to avoid the infamous "grandfather paradox" of the person who travels back in time to kill his or her ancestor, a paradox that has often been explored in science fiction. But it has also received seri-

---

26. Paul J. Nahin, *Time Machines* (New York: American Institute of Physics, 1993).

27. Kurt Gödel, "Example of a New Type of Cosmological Solution of Einstein's Field Equations of Gravitation," *Reviews of Modern Physics* 21 (1949): 447.

28. Kip S. Thorne, *Black Holes and Time Warps* (New York: W. W. Norton, 1994).

ous scientific and philosophical attention which has shown that time travel need not be self-contradictory.[29]

I have to emphasize that the possibilities of faster-than-light communication and time travel are at present entirely formal. We do not know if any of the phenomena that might reverse temporal order are realized in our world or, if they are, whether or how we might exploit them. It is possible that further scientific developments will make it possible to answer these questions and to develop technologies for genuine interstellar travel or time machines. I want to turn now, however, to the significance of these ideas for theology.

The Coming of the Future

In its creeds the church proclaims its belief that Christ will come to judge his world and establish the eternal kingdom — "We believe that you will come and be our judge," *Judex crederis esse venturus*, the *Te Deum* sings. This "coming" should be understood in the sense we discussed earlier, and not as an expectation that Christ will enter the universe from outside its spatial limits, whatever that might mean. It is an expression of the hope that God's ultimate future will come from the future, and it is based on the belief that a foretaste of that future has already burst into the middle of cosmic history in the first century on planet Earth with the resurrection of the crucified.

We have already noted that the conventional way of thinking about the world assumes that the present unfolds from the past in a more or less determinate way. This seems obvious, and it is often the assumptions that seem so obvious that they needn't be defended which need to be examined. With this way of thinking it is hard to imagine anything genuinely new, anything not already implicit in the conditions of the present, emerging in the future.[30] Even less does it seem possible that the present could be affected by the future. We can discover new historical or scientific information about the past, but to the extent that it is known, the past is fixed, like a museum exhibit. "The moving finger writes" and nothing that happens in the future

---

29. Nahin, *Time Machines*, ch. 4.

30. Cf. Eberhard Jüngel, "The Emergence of the New," in *Theological Essays II* (Edinburgh: T. & T. Clark, 1995).

can change what is written. That is why we think it appropriate to speak about "the dead past."

This is, however, a rather narrow view of relationships between future and past. To begin with, the future can have what we could call a *hermeneutical* influence on the past: It is in light of their future that we attach significance to events of the past. The American Civil War, whose effects are still felt in American society 140 years later, is also significant for our understanding of events *before* 1861: The slave trade, the national constitution, invention of the cotton gin, and the Missouri Compromise must all be seen in light of that conflict. In the New Testament, it is the resurrection of Jesus that illumines the "the law of Moses and the prophets and the psalms" (Luke 24:44) and the whole history of Israel. The relationship between the Old Testament and the Christ event is not one of simple prediction, but of meaning being put into the scriptures from their future.[31] And it is God's final future, "the Day of the Lord," that will show the significance of each person's life: "The work of each builder will become visible, for the Day will disclose it" (1 Cor. 3:13). The Christian claim is that ultimately the unfolding of all cosmic history since the big bang finds its meaning in the resurrection of the crucified as God's "plan for the fullness of time, to gather up all things in [Christ], things in heaven and things on earth" (Eph. 1:10).

The ideas arising from theoretical physics we have discussed suggest that we might be able to speak about an influence of the future on the past in a more concrete way as well. If cosmological repulsion is due to the pervasion of the universe by matter sustaining negative pressure, if advanced waves are real, or if exotic wormholes can be constructed, then physical signals and material bodies could conceivably travel backward in time. There could be a unique configuration of the universe at each cosmic time, but that configuration would be informed by its future as well as by its past. These provide ways in which a state of affairs in the future could exert a physical influence upon events in the past.

But before we speculate about ways in which such influences take place, we must remember that the eschaton is not to be thought of simply as a result of some novel properties of matter and space-time

31. Cf. Oscar Cullmann, *Christ and Time*, rev. ed. (Philadelphia: Westminster, 1954).

that science may be able to understand and technology to control. That would again be a process of collapsing eschatological tensions by making the future entirely continuous with the world that is accessible to present-day understanding. The value of any suggestions that can be made about faster-than-light communication, artificial intelligence, or any other scientific possibility is that they may serve as analogies for realities that cannot be described entirely in scientific terms. The understanding of the eschaton they may give can be only partial.

The use of analogies in order to make some sense of the inbreaking of the eschaton in the resurrection of Jesus goes back to the very beginnings of Christianity.[32] In 1 Corinthians 15 Paul insists that Jesus was truly raised from the dead and that there will be a general resurrection of which Christ is the "first fruits." But then he has to confront the challenge, "How are the dead raised? With what kind of body do they come?" How can the resurrection of the dead make any sense in terms of our present understanding of the world?

Paul's response is instructive. He begins by calling that person a "fool" who demands an answer to this question as a condition for faith. But then he goes on to answer the question, not with attempts to *prove* the resurrection but with analogies. He points out that different living things have different kinds of flesh, and that there are different types of bodies, terrestrial and celestial. Perhaps his most helpful analogy is that of the seed and the plant: There is both continuity and transformation, for the plant that grows is not identical with the seed that is buried. Examples from the present world help us to think about ways in which the new creation may be possible. Clement of Rome used not only Paul's example of the seed but also the story of the phoenix, which he and his contemporaries could read of in Herodotus or Pliny's *Natural History*, to argue for the resurrection.[33]

Paul's example of a seed growing into a plant is an illustrative analogy: The resurrection body is to the body that dies as the full-grown plant is to the seed. He certainly does not mean that a dead body will sprout and grow into a spiritual body as a plant does from a seed. Developments in modern physics that indicate the possibility of

32. George L. Murphy, "What Can Physics Contribute to Eschatology?" *dialog* 38 (1999): 35.

33. "The First Epistle of Clement to the Corinthians," vol. 1 of *The Ante-Nicene Fathers*, ed. Alexander Roberts and James Donaldson (Grand Rapids: Eerdmans, 1979), chs. 24 and 25.

communications and travel backward in time provide analogies that may be stronger than illustrations. Believing that God works through natural processes,[34] possibly also in many events that are considered miraculous, we can imagine how the phenomena to which modern physics seems to point are the kinds of things God *may* use in order to bring about the resurrection and eschatological fulfillment of creation.

We might give imagination free rein and suppose that an advanced technological civilization of the future will be able to gather a tremendous amount of information about some individual who has died in the past in order to run a perfect computer simulation of that person, complete with his or her life experience. This mental simulation could be combined with a genetic replica of that person through cloning technology in order to bring about a sort of resurrection. If this civilization also had the capability of faster-than-light signaling, it would be possible for this revivified person to be projected back in time to a period just following his or her death.[35] The resurrection of this person would then in a sense burst upon people of that time from the future.

Furthermore, the possibilities we have mentioned mean that the situation of life in the far future would be quite different from what would otherwise be expected. Faster-than-light travel would mean that the entirety of the universe would continue to be accessible in spite of the continually accelerating cosmic expansion.

All of this may sound like bizarre science fiction, and I stress again that the purpose of these speculations is only to suggest mechanisms that could give a hint of something like resurrection from the future and an eternal kingdom of God that includes our universe. The important point is that the universe may be open to divine action through natural processes to bring about the eschaton. We have in no way *explained* the resurrection of Christ or the parousia. Even if the possibili-

---

34. Robert John Russell, "Special Providence and Genetic Mutation: A New Defense of Theistic Evolution," in *Evolutionary and Molecular Biology,* ed. Robert John Russell, William R. Stoeger, and Francisco Ayala (Berkeley: Center for Theology and the Natural Sciences, 1998), p. 191; George L. Murphy, "The Theology of the Cross and God's Work in the World," *Zygon* 33 (1998): 221.

35. Some of the ideas here are suggested by C. J. Cherryh's science fiction novel *Cyteen* (New York: Warner, 1988) as well as by Tipler, *The Physics of Immortality.* See also George L. Murphy, "The End of History in the Middle: Speculation on the Resurrection," *Works* 5, no. 2 (1995): 1.

ties we have sketched become firmly established science, these concepts of Christian theology will not have become part of science.

In the first place, science would not explain the *particularity* of the historical resurrection, which is the prolepsis of the eschaton. To think of resurrection as the achievement of life after death for some arbitrary person through science-based technology would fall far short of the gospel. The Easter message is not just the resurrection of "someone" but of the particular person Jesus who died on the cross "under Pontius Pilate." "You are looking for Jesus of Nazareth, who was crucified. He has been raised; he is not here" (Mark 16:6).

This is a critical point, for if resurrection in the middle of history really is proleptic of God's final future, then the one who is raised shows the kind of future that God intends for the universe. The message that Nero had risen from the dead (which seems to have been a popular fear at the time the Book of Revelation was written) would be profoundly bad news.[36] The message that Jesus is risen is good news because it means that his life of total obedience to and trust in the Father and love for others is the ultimate future of the universe.

The resurrection of Jesus is seen in the New Testament not simply as a return to ordinary human life but as a passage to a life that is beyond death: "Death no longer has dominion over him" (Rom. 6:9). This is a promise of a transformation of our universe in which the vision of life beyond death in fellowship with God becomes a reality for all God's people and, indeed, for "all things." As those who are still in the middle of cosmic history but "on whom the end of the ages has come" (1 Cor. 10:11), we may be able to see in our present understanding of the world hints of how God will bring this about, and are encouraged to give further attention to the kinds of scientific possibilities that have been sketched here.

The Eschatological Presence of the Crucified

The suggestions we have made so far have to do primarily with the resurrection of Christ from the dead as the coming of God's ultimate

36. It has been suggested that popular fear of a return of Nero *redivivus* lies behind some of the imagery of the Book of Revelation. Cf. N. Turner, "Revelation," in *Peake's Commentary on the Bible*, ed. Matthew Black (New York: Thomas Nelson and Sons, 1962), sections 921g, 923e, 924a, e, & i.

future into the middle of cosmic history. But if we leave it at that our discussion is subject to the same criticism that we made of Tipler's eschatology, and indeed that could be made of most eschatological scenarios, religious or secular: It is just one more theology of glory. By describing a way in which the resurrection is made real, we might be seen as assigning the cross to the dead past, and that will not do. Easter is the resurrection of the one who died on the cross. Paul's insistence that he had been intent on proclaiming only "Christ crucified" (1 Cor. 2:2) in the same letter in which he speaks in detail about the resurrection in chapter 15 makes it clear that the risen Christ must always be identified as the crucified.

There is another aspect of physics that is suggestive of ways to approach this important theme, the Second Law of Thermodynamics. While the First Law says that the total energy of a closed system cannot be changed, the Second Law says that the amount of that energy which is available for the performance of useful work can never increase, and that for realistic processes it will in fact *decrease*. Any heat engine eventually runs down. The Second Law can also be stated in another way in terms of what goes on at the molecular level: A system of molecules always tends toward more probable statistical distributions in position and velocity. Since highly ordered states are relatively unlikely, this means that the Second Law can be seen as a "law of increasing disorder." In a more formal way, the entropy of a state of a system is defined in terms of the probability of that state, and the Second Law says that the entropy of a closed system can never decrease and will generally increase.[37]

Both these ways of stating the Second Law mean that there is an asymmetry between past and future, so that an arrow of time can be defined. Time increases in the direction in which heat flows spontaneously from hot regions to cold, a drop of ink diffuses outward into a glass of water, or a wheel spinning on an axle slows down due to friction. We simply do not see these processes happening in the opposite way as we move forward in time.

More pointedly, the increase of time is marked by motion from life to death. Biological organisms are heat engines (though not "merely heat engines" as simplistic reductionists would say) that make use of

---

37. See, e.g., Edward A. Desloge, *Thermal Physics* (New York: Holt, Rinehart and Winston, 1968), pp. 24-57.

the energy stored in the chemical bonds of organic molecules. Eventually these engines run down and stop. After death our bodies come apart. The "corruption" that was such a feared enemy in the Greek thought taken over by the fathers of the Eastern church, a consequence of the compound character of things, can to some extent be identified with the tendency described by the Second Law.[38]

The disorder and dying associated with entropy suggest that there is some connection between this thermodynamic variable and the presence of natural evil in the world.[39] But we cannot simply identify entropy with evil. Without the tendency described by the Second Law the kinds of changes possible in the world would only be simple "reversible processes"[40] that can be undone as easily as they are done. As simple a process as the coming to a common temperature of a hot and a cold glass of water when they are poured into the same container is irreversible, leading to an increase in entropy. And most importantly, life would not be possible if it were not for the growth of entropy. The chemical processes of the metabolisms of living things depend in fundamental ways on the tendency described by the Second Law.

Modern thermodynamics has moved from the classical study of equilibrium situations to treatment of irreversible or nonequilibrium thermodynamics, and in doing so has revealed some qualitatively new possibilities.[41] In the past it seemed natural to associate the growth of entropy with the running down and coming apart of things, with the "Change and decay in all around I see" of the popular hymn.[42] But nonequilibrium thermodynamics reveals that the growth of entropy may be connected with, and even thought of as generating, structures in open systems. A simple example is provided by the convection cells that form in a layer of fluid when its top and bottom are kept at different temperatures so that heat flows irreversibly between them. Detailed geometric patterns formed by systems of chemical reactions are another instance. These are referred to as "dissipative structures" be-

---

38. George L. Murphy, "Time, Thermodynamics, and Theology," *Zygon* 26 (1991): 359.

39. Robert John Russell, "Entropy and Evil," *Zygon* 19 (1984): 449.

40. Desloge, *Thermal Physics*, pp. 27-30.

41. E.g., Ilya Prigogine, *From Being to Becoming* (New York: W. H. Freeman, 1980).

42. Henry F. Lyte, "Abide with Me," *Lutheran Book of Worship* (Minneapolis: Augsburg, 1978), Hymn #272, v. 3.

cause they accompany the dissipation of energy, the loss of capacity for useful work, which the Second Law describes.[43]

Biological organisms are of course much more complex than a layer of fluid or a mixture of a few chemical compounds, but one of their essential features is that they are not in thermodynamic equilibrium with their environments. Life depends upon there being flows of energy and matter through the organism. (Thus "to assume room temperature" is a euphemism for "to die.") It is possible to think of living things as very complex dissipative structures, remaining alive only when accompanied by the continual generation of entropy. In other words, entropy has an essential role in the development and maintenance of life.

If we search for theological parallels to these concepts, it is not difficult to see connections with the Christian belief in the relationships between death and life that are centered on the cross-resurrection complex. Death is not seen in the New Testament in a Stoic or Platonic way: Paul's description of it as "the last enemy to be destroyed" (1 Cor. 15:26) gives a very different image from that of Socrates' death in the *Phaedo,* and the death of Christ is death in its worst form, *mors turpissima crucis,* brought about by human moral evil and due, in theological analysis, to the weight of human sin in the world. Yet the New Testament describes this particular death as the source of life. The Gospel of Matthew (27:52-53) pictures this with an image of the opening of tombs and the raising of the saints when Jesus dies on the cross.

Christ is risen beyond the bounds of death, but this does not mean that he is isolated from suffering. Matthew's parable of the last judgment (Matt. 25:31-46) speaks of the identification of the Son of Man with those who suffer hunger, sickness, and other privations. The account of Paul's conversion experience, in which the risen Christ speaks of *himself* being persecuted by the enemy of the church, has been seen as the origin of the Pauline concept of the church as the Body of Christ,[44] a super-personal entity that has an eschatological goal, as we see especially in the Letter to the Ephesians. Teilhard de Chardin suggested that just as the coming together of individual cells to form multicellular organisms was a crucial step in biological evolu-

43. Prigogine, *From Being to Becoming,* pp. 77-128.
44. John A. T. Robinson, *The Body* (Philadelphia: Westminster, 1952), p. 58.

tion, the bringing together of individual persons in the Body of Christ should be seen as the future of the evolutionary process.[45]

The Body of Christ continues to suffer while it is the means through which God works to bring the world to the eschatological fulfillment that has already been seen in the resurrection. It is "always carrying about in the body the death of Jesus, so that the life of Jesus may also be made visible in our bodies" (2 Cor. 4:10). In this sense we might speak of the Body of which Christ is the head as the "ultimate dissipative structure." The cross continues to mark the development of the world toward the eschaton, the resurrection.

Eadem Mutata Resurgo

The hope of resurrection is for fulfillment of the lives we know by transformation into something of which we have only hints, and that is a hope we are given not only for our individual lives but for the entire creation. The mathematician Jakob Bernoulli expressed this hope in the inscription that he asked to have placed on his tombstone, an inscription that offers one more analogy in closing. It showed the curve called the logarithmic spiral, which appears in many guises in mathematics, with the words *eadem mutata resurgo*, "I arise the same though changed."[46]

---

45. Pierre Teilhard de Chardin, *Christianity and Evolution* (New York: Harcourt Brace Jovanovich, 1969), pp. 16 and 66-72.

46. Dirk J. Struik, *A Concise History of Mathematics*, 2nd rev. ed. (New York: Dover, 1948), p. 165.

Contributors

CARL E. BRAATEN, Executive Director, Center for Catholic and Evangelical Theology; Co-editor of *Pro Ecclesia, A Journal of Catholic and Evangelical Theology*, Sun City West, Arizona

PAUL D. HANSON, Professor of Old Testament, The Divinity School, Harvard University, Cambridge, Massachusetts

ARLAND J. HULTGREN, Professor of New Testament, Luther Seminary, St. Paul, Minnesota

ROBERT W. JENSON, Senior Scholar for Research, Center of Theological Inquiry, Princeton, New Jersey; Co-editor of *Pro Ecclesia, A Journal of Catholic and Evangelical Theology*

PHILIP D. KREY, President and Professor of Early Church History, Lutheran Theological Seminary, Philadelphia, Pennsylvania

JOHN A. McGUCKIN, Professor of Early Church History, Union Theological Seminary, New York, New York

GEORGE L. MURPHY, Pastoral Associate, St. Paul's Episcopal Church, Akron, Ohio; and Adjunct Faculty Member, Trinity Lutheran Seminary, Columbus, Ohio

DAVID NOVAK, Professor and Director of the Jewish Studies Program, University of Toronto, Toronto, Canada

WOLFHART PANNENBERG, Professor of Systematic Theology, University of Munich, Munich, Germany

169